Strategic
Relations Leadership

Public relations is operating in an increasingly challenging and complex environment. Pressures from outside the organisation include new accountabilities, empowered stakeholders, increased public cynicism and a new communication landscape. Internally, there are increasing demands to demonstrate a return on investment, alongside a requirement to coach and counsel senior managers exposed to these environmental pressures.

This context requires public relations professionals to be able to clearly articulate and demonstrate their own contribution to organisational effectiveness. This textbook provides public relations leaders with a framework to do this, as well as a checklist of essential capabilities which they must acquire and exhibit if they are to operate at the highest levels of any organisation.

This short textbook is suitable for aspiring practitioners, MBA and other masters qualifications in public relations – especially for those students who wish to pursue a successful career as a professional PR specialist able to operate strategically at the top of successful organisations.

Anne Gregory is Professor of Public Relations and Director of the Centre for Public Relations Studies, at Leeds Metropolitan University, UK, and Chair of the Global Alliance.

Paul Willis is Director of the Centre for Public Relations Studies at Leeds Metropolitan University, UK.

Strategic Public Relations Leadership

Anne Gregory and Paul Willis

Routledge
Taylor & Francis Group

LONDON AND NEW YORK

First published 2013
by Routledge
2 Park Square, Milton Park, Abingdon, Oxon OX14 4RN

Simultaneously published in the USA and Canada
by Routledge
711 Third Avenue, New York, NY 10017

Routledge is an imprint of the Taylor & Francis Group, an informa business

British Library Cataloguing in Publication Data
A catalogue record for this book is available from the British Library

Library of Congress Cataloging in Publication Data
Gregory, Anne, 1953-
Strategic public relations leadership / Anne Gregory and Paul Willis.
pages cm
Includes bibliographical references and index.
1. Public relations--Management. I. Willis, Paul A. II. Title.
HD59.G687 2013
659.2--dc23
2012045629

ISBN: 978-0-415-66794-4 (hbk)
ISBN: 978-0-415-66795-1 (pbk)
ISBN: 978-0-203-38473-2 (ebk)

Typeset in Times New Roman
by Saxon Graphics Ltd, Derby

MIX
Paper from
responsible sources
FSC
www.fsc.org   FSC® C013056

Printed and bound in Great Britain by
TJ International Ltd, Padstow, Cornwall

From Anne: to those who I love and who love me

From Paul to Joanna: thanks for listening, I know how hard that can be sometimes!

Contents

PART III
The responsibilities of public relations leaders 101

Figures

Tables

Acknowledgements

We would like to acknowledge the many colleagues and fellow professionals who have helped us in our public relations careers for their wisdom and encouragement.

There are a number of people who have been particularly important to us while developing this book. Thanks to Colin Douglas, former Director of Communications for the UK National Health Service, and two other directors from the NHS, Steph Hood and Karl Milner. Thank you too to Alex Aiken, Executive Director of Government Communications, as well as the other outstanding professionals in the UK Cabinet Office and government departments who have shared their challenges and issues with us. We owe a tremendous debt to fellow professionals from around the world in companies and universities on every continent who have listened to us patiently, bettered our thinking and shared their knowledge. Gratitude is also due to our past and existing clients from both the private and public sector with whom we have shared both the thrill and frustrations of public relations practice. These experiences have also helped to guide and shape the content of the book. Our Executive Masters students have been a source of inspiration and pride to us, and willing guinea pigs for our ideas as we have developed them. Numerous academic colleagues have challenged, cursed and blessed us in equal measure, and our particular thanks go to David McKie and Margalit Toledano for their inspiration and for standing with us.

Anne would like to thank Paul for being a great colleague, friend and co-toiler without whose questions, answers, rapier insights, good humour and copious cups of tea this book would never have been written.

Paul would like to thank Anne for her unstinting encouragement and expert guidance not just in the production of this book but also as his mentor and friend. Paul also wishes to acknowledge his wife Joanna for her support, patience and insights on the early drafts.

1 Introduction

Aims, aspirations and approach

Life as a public relations practitioner is challenging. Taking on the role of an organisational leader is also fraught with issues and this has generated a mountain of books and scholarly articles. In this book we want to take a long, hard look at bringing these two roles together. Our aim is to provide a leadership framework that works for public relations. We believe this way of looking at leadership is applicable whether public relations leaders work in the private, public or third sector.[1] By the end of the book it should also become clear that what makes people effective public relations professionals can make them a good leader. As a result, we also suggest that the book's key insights will be of use to chief executives and other senior managers, as well as those who have a specific responsibility for public relations.

Our guiding star when writing each chapter has to been to generate insights that will be of use in practice. Both of us are former practitioners and as academics we continue to work with organisations not only as consultants, but as people who are regularly seconded into the workplace to work with practitioners on real issues. These issues are often around public relations leadership and how to develop leaders. Our preoccupation with the day-to-day challenges facing public relations leaders is important as it can appear as if public relations academics and practitioners inhabit different worlds, or as Betteke van Ruler (2005) poetically put it, 'professionals are from Venus and scholars are from Mars'.[2] The thinking put forward in the book matches our own experiences as practitioners, as well as those of the senior professionals we work with. Indeed, our ideas are the product of many years as professionals in leadership positions ourselves and of discussions, joint projects and research with public relations leaders from a wide range of organisations and sectors, both in the UK and in every continent around the world. The views and opinions of those who toil at the coalface has been a crucial test in shaping the book's content. Indeed, we think much more should be done to involve practitioners and researchers in co-created learning.

In our view, too little attention is paid to the knowledge that practitioners bring to the table and the productive role this can play in research and professional education. This conclusion has been re-enforced by the privilege we have had in developing an Executive Masters programme for public relations leaders the content of which is co-created by them, their chief executives, other key organisational stakeholders and us as educators.[3] However, who is educating who is a moot point and the insights generated from this challenging process continue to stimulate our thinking on public relations leadership and has helped to shape the content of this book. We hope, therefore, that what follows is a realistic and practical perspective on the role of the public relations leader. As authors we have been careful to avoid just describing the world as it should be, rather than as it is.

It is important to emphasise that this practical focus has not resulted in a technical, 'how to' manual for professionals. Rather our intention is to provide a strategic lens through which practitioners can view their role as public relations leaders. This will allow them to verbalise, reflect on and demonstrate their contribution to organisational effectiveness. Every organisation is different, so we have specifically designed the lens to be varifocal – applicable to any kind of organisation. Our ambition is that these insights should have immediate applicability for those operating at board level and/or heading up a public relations department, as well as ring bells with and provide a target for people who aspire to such positions.

Although the public relations leadership model and the roles it defines put forward here is original, we suspect its most important role will be to articulate what many public relations professionals already know and do intuitively. This has certainly been a recurring theme in our discussions with practitioners over the years and has proved valuable to them. In this regard the book will help to systemise thinking and enable public relations leaders to explain better why their contribution is a strategic asset for the organisation.

Having made this strategic case, our focus on key aspects of leadership and on behaviours and capabilities shows how practitioners can go about enacting this role. This discussion will challenge the reader to shape their own development by applying the book's key insights to their own situation. It is worth noting that some key themes such as contextual intelligence, organisational purpose, values and leadership itself are recurrent themes that knit much of the book together.

The shape of the book

The book is structured into three parts. Part I looks at the strategic contribution that public relations makes to organisations. Chapter 2 first defines the nature of organisations and then looks at organisations from a public relations standpoint comparing this with the more well-known management and stakeholder perspectives. It concludes that viewing the organisation through a public relations lens can bring special insights and lays on it responsibilities and opportunities that are particularly pertinent in the modern world. Leadership is covered in Chapter 3 where we highlight the common ground between public relations and leadership as strategic processes. Chapter 4 looks at the challenging role of the chief executive in the modern world and how public relations leaders are helping them address the new accountabilities they face. Chapter 5 forms the heart of the whole book. In it we describe the four-by-four model which clarifies the strategic contribution of public relations at four levels in the organisation and propose four attributes which characterise public relations work at all these levels. Falling out of this model, we articulate four roles for the public relations leader which will place them at the very centre of the organisation.

Part II looks at the preoccupations of the public relations leader. Chapter 6 examines the importance of the public relations leader as the guru of contextual intelligence. This is not just about relying on formal systems to bring intelligence into the organisation, but about a strategic mindset that can embrace uncertainty and ambiguity and draw strategic insights from it. This leads very naturally to Chapter 7 and a discussion on values. The centrality of an authentic set of values for the organisation, and the role of the public relations leader in helping to define, develop and embed those values is seen to be vital to organisational health. The twin chapter of values is Chapter 8, ethics. The importance of ethics as fundamental to the building of trust, a snapshot of some ethical traditions, linking ethics to leadership and a model for ethical decision-making, constitute the bulk of this chapter. This then sets the context for Chapter 9 on the behaviours, or competencies that are intrinsic to the role of the public relations leader. Using original research[4] with public relations leaders at board level, this chapter describes the crucial behaviours that need to be learned and demonstrated by practitioners in the private and public sectors.

In Part III we look at a number of responsibilities that the public relations leader needs to shoulder as well as providing more detail on two of the roles outlined in Chapter 5, those of catalyst and implementer (or, to use the chapter title, expert technician). Part III begins with Chapter 10 which identifies strategic planning as a core capability and preoccupation of the public relations leader. It explains how planning principles can be applied at the four levels of the four-by-four model and tackles some of the problems that seem to be endemic in public relations planning such as framing objectives and evaluation.

The four-by-four model introduces the idea of the public relations leader as catalyst and Chapter 11 explores this concept in detail. This role requires the public relations leader to be involved in the structures, processes and systems of the organisation because every element tells its own story and organisational narrative is the territory of public relations. Although this book is about strategic leadership, Chapter 12 makes no apology for focusing on the technician role, but from a different angle. The notion of expertise comes to the fore here, and is used to highlight how the technical capability of leaders is quite different from less experienced colleagues. Expertise brings a leader credibility both within the public relations leader's department and within the organisation. Implicit within the concept of leadership, is the sense that leaders can be learned from, so Chapter 13 opens up the idea of the public relations leader as internal educator, embedding communication literacy throughout the organisation and coaching managers and others to undertake technical tasks. Part III rounds up with a chapter on the consultancy mindset. It proposes that public relations leaders should work as consultants at all levels in the organisation, maintaining the objectivity and independence that consultants are assiduous in developing and defending. The tensions of being an organisational leader while also being detached is one of the key challenges that face senior practitioners, but it is also a measure of their worth.

The book finishes with our view of the future. However, we do not want to be predictable by taking out our crystal ball and pontificating about the future. In our view the future is quite unknown. The last five years have been phenomenal for public relations with the rise of all sorts of technologies and channels which were not even dreamt of. All we can be certain about is that change will be faster and even more profound. However, we conclude by making the bold claim that the capabilities that we describe in this book will remain the same whatever the future holds. The nature of leadership including public relations leadership is constant; it is just the context that changes.

We trust this book is stimulating and that the insights that we have gained from many colleagues over the years and which have prompted us to think in new ways proves to be of help to those who aspire to be strategic public relations leaders.

Notes

1   The third sector comprises non-government organisations such as voluntary organisations, charities, social enterprises, community groups, cooperatives and mutual associations.
2   Van Ruler, B. (2005). Commentary: professionals are from Venus, scholars are from Mars, *Public Relations Review*, 31, 159–73.
3   For a discussion of the thinking and process behind the Masters see Willis, P. and McKie, D. (2011). Outsourcing public relations pedagogy: lessons from innovation, management futures and stakeholder participation. *Public Relations Review*, 37(3), 466–9.
4   Gregory, A. (2008). The competencies of senior practitioners in the UK: an initial study, *Public Relations Review*, 34(3), 215–23.

Part I

The strategic contribution of public relations

In Part I of this book we look at four key elements which we believe make up the strategic contribution of public relations in organisations.

To set the context we look at the organisation from a public relations perspective. Finance directors see their organisations through a financial lens, human resources (HR) directors through an HR lens: we believe there is also a public relations lens which brings a powerful dimension to the strategic toolkit of senior executives. First of all we discuss what an organisation is; we then look at some of the insights that we can gain from general management (including the latest thinking on stakeholders); and then we turn to the public relations perspective and spend some time examining how public relations can enable the organisation to achieve its objectives. However, we then go on to claim that organisations are actually constituted through communications; they are what they communicate.

The second element of Part I explores leadership and public relations. Here we draw parallels between what is generally recognised as the key traits of leadership and what public relations practitioners are expected to do. We observe that there is a remarkable correspondence between these two: to be a senior public relations practitioner requires leadership capability.

Our third topic examines how public relations can support the chief executive. We look at how the public relations lens can help the chief executive to understand a world that requires increasing levels of accountability and transparency. We also observe the need for the public relations leader to attach to the chief executive's agenda and to help them in problem-solving. We find that the public relations professional is uniquely qualified to do this.

To complete Part I we introduce a new model of strategic public relations which we call the four-by-four model. This model describes the contribution that public relations can make at four strategic levels within any organisation. It then proposes four key attributes which should characterise public relations at whatever level it is being undertaken. We call these the DNA strands because like DNA they permeate and form the core of public relations practice. This model has led us to conclude that there are four key roles for the public relations leader: the orienter, the navigator, the catalyst and the implementer.

Part 1

The strategic contribution
of public relations

2 A public relations view of the organisation

Most business specialisms have a particular lens through which they see their organisation. Lawyers view organisations as legally constituted entities of various kinds and are concerned with legal processes. Accountants see organisations as collections of resources that can be marshalled to support business objectives. But is there a public relations lens through which to see organisations? This chapter will explore this question by examining four areas:

- What an organisation is
- A management perspective
- A stakeholder perspective
- A public relations perspective

What an organisation is

The academic and popular literature on 'organisations' is vast[1] and it is not the purpose of this chapter to try to summarise it. However, a number of themes helped to frame our thinking about a public relations perspective.

First, it is obvious that there are many kinds of organisation: public, private, not-for-profit; local, national and global; and based in or serving many different industry sectors. These factors affect organisational *purpose*, which will be addressed later in this chapter.

Second, organisations are often seen as economic units, either generating income and profits, or working within budgets provided by other people. In the present economic climate, efficiency is an area of focus; indeed as Antonio Tencati and Laszlo Zsolnai[2] put it, 'economic efficiency has become the greatest source of social legitimacy for business'.

Third, organisations are not just economic units or collections of resources, but 'actors' in the social sphere. They help shape culture: think of Coca-Cola, Nike, Facebook, Greenpeace and the US Army. They affect the way people live and organise their lives. What they do has social implications; for example, if a large organisation moves away from an area there are usually social impacts. Business thinking has affected the way society has developed and is deeply embedded in the Western psyche, with consumerist and cost/benefit norms being prevalent.

Fourth, organisations have multiple identities:[3] these are perceived by the different types of interactions people and groups have with them although there is considerable debate about whether organisations should try to project one unified or uniform identity despite this.[4]

Finally, organisations are organic, evolving and deeply relational. They are usually made up of people, although some organisations have very few, but facilitate connections between people, for example Twitter. Organisations interact with others. They create connections and conversations; indeed, authors such as Linda Putnam and Anne Nicotera[5] would claim that organisations are constituted by communication: they cannot exist without it. 'Organising' happens as people communicate and undertake action.

A management perspective

Again, there are libraries of literature on how managers view their organisations and, just a few strands are drawn out here for consideration.

Even in today's web 2.0 and soon-to-be Web 3.0 networked world, most managers, when they draw a stakeholder map, will put the organisation in the centre of it with stakeholders, like satellites, set in its ambit of influence. However, in a network society an organisation is just one node in a network, not at the centre because, by their very nature, networks do not have centres. This is a salutary truth: organisations may be in the centre of some people's and groups networks, but for most they are not. They are at the centre of a number of nodes of equal if not more importance, such as family, friends, leisure activities and other intellectual interests.

A dominant management theory and one that takes up much management thinking is the gaining of competitive advantage.[6] The pursuit of a favourable position in relation to competitors is multifaceted and not only includes attracting more customers, but also skilled staff, financial support and/or social acceptability. Competitive advantage applies equally to private, public or not-for-profit organisations. Public-sector organisations compete for more budget vis-à-vis other public-sector organisations and not-for-profit organisations compete for funding, volunteers and approval from supporters.

There are many theories about how competitive advantage can be gained, but one that has currency at the moment is the resource-based view (RBV) of organisations.[7] RBV sees organisations as 'bundles of resources' which, if configured and strategically deployed, provide a unique competency base which is rare, non-substitutable, difficult to imitate and of value and this is a source of competitive advantage. One of the components in this unique competency base is corporate identity. Marlena Fiol[8] first recognised the potential of a strong corporate identity (now often called corporate brand) to create value and from this the concept of reputational resource has gained attention and credence. Business leaders recognise the significance of reputational assets, often realised when an organisation is valued by markets, or sold. In a recent valuation of its brand, Coca-Cola estimated that 87 per cent of its value was in intangibles.[9] Intangibles are largely based on the ability of the organisation to attract support because it is seen to provide *value* in various forms. This value can be seen as *capital* which enables the organisation to gain influence – which of course also provides competitive advantage. The French sociologist Pierre Bourdieu[10] states that this influence can be exercised in four overlapping areas of resources: economic, that is control over assets; social, having connections to others who will support; cultural, the organisation has socially desirable goods; and symbolic, because others acknowledge the organisation's status and prestige. Some organisations, with Apple being a prescient example, have acquired influence in all four of these areas and competitive success is apparent.

A stakeholder perspective

Stakeholders, including customers, can be viewed in the same light: as resources or potential assets. They are potentially sources of intelligence, can generate ideas for new products and can be advocates for the organisation. The Harley Owners Group (HOG) have been significantly influential in the development, survival and product innovations of Harley-Davidson. An alternative and more pessimistic view of stakeholders is that they are potentially a problem in that they can get in the way or slow down management aspirations by opposing or questioning. If they do, organisations may incur additional costs and potentially be forced to change course which may be expensive. Major public opposition to genetically modified (GM) foods led by a number of activist groups in Europe has delayed the introduction of GM products significantly and blocked the attendant profit lines for several years.

When stakeholders are seen as potential resources or costs, both of these views can be seen to be relatively instrumental. Stakeholders are seen either as a way to achieve competitive advantage or as a group to be persuaded or silenced so that the organisation can 'get on with its business'. The fourth section of this chapter will return to this theme.

The classic definition of stakeholders is that they are made up of those individuals or groups that can affect or be affected by an organisation.[11] The definition's simplicity belies its complexity. It does not indicate how *much* of a stake a group or individual has, the amount of *time* the stake involves, the *risks* attached to it or the intrinsic *nature* of the stake. A sole family breadwinner who has a full-time job in an area of high unemployment has a very different stake from a remote investor who has a 0.5 per cent of her considerable wealth staked in the organisation. Furthermore, situations often dictate the nature of the stake taken in an organisation. A regular user of bank services may well be quite passive until something happens such as a threat to the service. James Grunig[12] says that stakeholders tend to become active when three conditions are satisfied:

- they recognise that an issue or problem exists;
- there are no real constraints to their taking action; and
- they are personally and emotionally involved and affected.

For all but those most closely involved in an organisation, their world is not organised around interactions with it. They dip in and out of relationships with it, and even if contact is regular the relationship may be purely transactional. Shopping at a supermarket is typically of this nature. A transactional relationship means that an organisation has something that an individual or group supports, desires or needs and they will exchange something for it whether that be money, time, taxes or talents. Certainly, most people do not regard themselves as a 'resource' of an organisation. They will engage with it for a number of reasons, maybe transactional, but also because it may satisfy a range of needs and desires, some of which may be about generating self-esteem and some may be altruistic. Indeed, all levels of Maslow's[13] famous hierarchy of needs given in Figure 2.1 can be addressed by the range of organisations with whom individuals interact.

What can be concluded from this section is that while organisations may have relatively straightforward reasons for wishing or needing to be engaged with stakeholders, the reasons why stakeholders wish to engage with organisations are multivariate and sometimes deeply complex. At one extreme the stake may be distant and lightly held; at the other the organisation itself becomes intimately bound up with an individual's self-identity. The clothing, music and prized possessions of street gangs being a case in point.

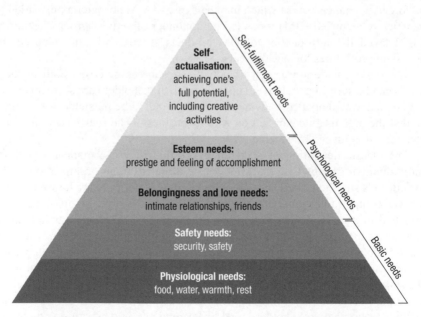

Figure 2.1 Maslow's hierarchy of needs with the most basic being at the lowest level

In the light of the foregoing, how, then, is a public relations perspective of organisations to be conceptualised?

A public relations perspective

It is important to define what is meant by public relations. We, along with others,[14] take the wide view: it involves all those deliberate efforts to formally communicate with individuals or groups and includes management or internal communication, marketing and advertising, and public relations. Public relations itself covers media (traditional, online and social), corporate communication, public affairs, community relations and investor relations. These disciplines are converging with each using the channels of the other and the drive for a more unified voice[15] makes it sensible pragmatically to bring them together. Communication is the word often used to describe these collective specialist functions, but we will use the phrase public relations because it best describes what happens: the organisation builds relationships in public and with these various publics.

The key thing about public relations is that it is, in effect, functionally neutral, or alternatively it can be regarded as functionally integrated; that is, it does not take any specialist business discipline perspective. For example, financial directors see organisations as bundles of resources, while operations directors see organisations through business process and structure lenses. The public relations leader's job is to see the organisation as a whole, with a helicopter view, seeing it held in the nexus of connections that make up its network, seeing it in context and, more specifically, seeing it as stakeholders see it. Public relations, because its raison d'être is to be 'publicly relating' internally and externally is uniquely placed to take this perspective. It is one of the few specialisms whose role is to be functionally neutral and indeed it is important that it remains so because if it does not, it loses its ability to take a multi-stakeholder perspective of the organisation. In this respect it is almost unique in the organisation. Indeed, it could be argued that apart from the chief executive the public relations leader is the only one with this holistic view and this is one reason why senior public relations executives often have a very close relationship with their chief executive. They are the ones who challenge decisions, asking whether consideration has been given to the possible reactions of certain stakeholder groups and whether all factors have been taken into account.

This book is about strategic public relations leadership, so the tactics and content of communication will not be covered in any depth. It is important however, to state unequivocally that the communication tactics and content an organisation uses are of ultimate importance. They provide both the concrete, physical 'texts'[16] (such as advertisements, websites and policies) and figurative or mental texts, such as the ingrained ways of working that characterise the culture and DNA of the organisation and which ultimately help to define the organisation itself.

The remainder of this chapter focuses on a public relations view of the organisation and it will look first at strategy contribution and second at stakeholder orientation.

The strategy contribution

Within organisations public relations is often seen in a support capacity. It is there to enable[17] the organisation to achieve its objectives: it is a resource to be used by senior managers and an asset to be exploited – which indeed it is. Thus, seeing the organisation as others see it, and obtaining information from the outside environment about trends and particularly about the attitudes and likely actions of stakeholders, is a key activity which helps managers make informed decisions. Similarly, projecting a particular corporate identity or brand, leading the efforts to protect the brand in a crisis, reaching-out proactively to stakeholders, and building communication processes and practices within the organisation are all valuable and essential parts of the enabling role (more of this in Chapter 5).

However, the public relations perspective does not stop at enabling. To realise its full potential, public relations also has a *constitutive* dimension. Enabling facilitates what is already there: the constitutive elements of an organisation are those things that must be present for it to exist in the first place and for it to endure into the future.

In practice, leaders determine a strategy which will help the organisation realise its objectives. Strategy-making is a communicative act. It is not a thing done in isolation, but in conversations between senior peers. Indeed the process of decision-making may well involve a range of people not only senior managers, but also external experts, internal advisers and employees. It will incorporate intelligence brought in through analyses and from various sources, including that brought in by public relations professionals in their enabling role. The way these decisions are made are through communication. Their content, the process undertaken to arrive at them, what is included and what is left out determines the very nature of the organisation and constitute what the organisation *is*. These decisions in themselves are communicative; that is, they tell a story about the organisation because usually different decisions could have been taken. That *those* decisions were made rather than other ones *is* the story. Furthermore until those decisions are communicated, they do not exist as propositions to be supported or disapproved of. In this way communication *is* organisation, not just *about* an organisation. This understanding is not just philosophical semantics. The reason the public relations perspective is so critically important is because it goes to the heart of how an organisation is recognised in the world. It is recognised when people can communicate about it and what they say is a matter of life and death for it.

The constitutive process of decision-making just alluded to in the previous paragraph is critical. First-order decisions address basic questions such as: What is our place in the world? What do we stand for? What will we do? How will we gain and marshal our resources to achieve what we would like to do? Who do we need to interact with to meet our goals? How do we know when we have succeeded?

All these questions are valued laden and have communication at their heart since to be successful, in whatever terms the organisation classifies success, is dependent on gaining the consent and support of other people – or stakeholders – who will have to detect *value* in what the organisation stands for and does. To gain that consent will require relationship-building and trust in the organisation, this latter being an essential element of organisational reputation. As this chapter has already indicated, value can have multiple interpretations depending on the nature of the stake in question. For some it will be financial, for others it will be social, for yet more it will be that the organisation fails.

A major task for senior managers to undertake, therefore, is to determine how their organisations are to be constituted: to determine what its DNA will be and what it will stand for. This is captured and embodied by the value-base of the organisation (more of this in Chapter 7). The value-base is the principal building block of the organisation: it determines the parameters of decision-making, helps to define and characterise it, will determine the stakeholders whose support is essential, the enemies that will be made and will be the basis for making judgements about organisational performance. Declared values are the touchstone of authenticity and because they are decided by the organisation itself, the ultimate test of its integrity. The distance between declared values and the 'lived experience' of stakeholders determines the legitimately gap. The public relations perspective finds that gap abhorrent because therein lies the principal reputation threat since relationships are put at risk.

The stakeholder contribution

From a public relations point of view, the way organisations interact with their stakeholders *is* the organisational narrative. This is quite different from the usual view of organisational narrative which is that it is something that is decided internally and then projected externally. This is wrong. The narrative consists of those conversations and actions with and by which stakeholders are engaged. It goes without saying, but how organisations think about their stakeholders will determine the nature of their engagement and how they prioritise their stakeholders. So, if stakeholders are regarded as a resource, a target or a cost, a particular approach will be taken. If they are regarded as collaborators, equals and as representative of an organisation's obligations to society, the interaction will be quite different. Indeed, the very act of defining stakeholder (although that is becoming increasingly difficult in a globalised, technologically enabled world) implies a particular understanding of the relationship. Their prioritisation has not only organisational and pragmatic implications, but ethical and moral dimensions because prioritisation involves judgements about importance and that is usually followed by resource allocation, with most time and money being given to those who are most important.

The prevailing mantra of much received wisdom is that stakeholder communication should be kept simple – the KISS acronym, Keep It Simple Stupid, encapsulates this thinking. This may indeed be quite adequate for those many stakeholders who only wish a superficial relationship with the organisation. However it is deeply damaging and insulting to those who legitimately wish for more. Rich and complex conversations build enduring and rewarding relationships with stakeholders and enduring relationships form the basis of the long-term sustainability of the organisation. Of course, the motives behind and nature of stakeholder engagement is a communicative act, not only in itself, but in what it implies about the values and priorities of the organisation.

To conclude this chapter it is necessary to draw together the threads of thinking that have been developed here. Organisations are more than economic units. They are social actors, have cultural influence and are symbolic of modern Western society. They are intrinsically communicative and create conversations. Senior managers lead purposive entities who deploy resources, including public relations to achieve their objectives. Stakeholders interact with organisations for many reasons and, for most, particular organisations are not the focal part of their lives.

Summary

A public relations perspective of the organisation sees it from a non-functional or integrated view: as a node in a network of communicative relationships which both define the organisation's place but also constitute its very self and meaning. The role of public relations is not only as an enabler, but as a constitutive part of an organisation. Without public relations there is no interaction because organisations do not exist in a vacuum. A key contribution for public relations is to help the organisation to determine its purpose, founded on an authentic value-base which is defining of the organisation and puts it in a place where it is ready to communicate with stakeholders. (For more on how this value-base can be collaboratively developed see Chapter 7.) The nature of the relationship with stakeholders forms the organisational narrative, which in turn builds value capital and the legitimacy on which the organisation builds its 'licence to operate'. An organisation's reputation is determined not by expert publicity programs, but the alignment of declared and enacted values as judged by those with whom it has a relationship. It is a public relations perspective that contributes the insight and understanding of these issues and its profound importance is signified by the fact that if the organisation gets these things wrong, it will cease to exist.

Notes

1 There are many standard management texts which provide overviews of the management and organisational literature, for example Johnson, G., Whittington, R. and Scholes, K. (2010). *Exploring Corporate Strategy*, 9th edition, Harlow: FT

Prentice Hall; Grant, R.M. (2010). *Contemporary Strategy Analysis*, 7th edition, Maldon, MA: Wiley-Blackwell; and de Wit, R. and Mayer, R. (2010). *Strategy Process, Content, Context*, 4th edition, Andover: South–Western CENGAGE Learning. Organisational studies looks at organisations as internally constituted entities. The book by Pugh D.S. and Hickson D.J., (2007) *Writers on Organisations*. London: Sage, brings together a selection of the best-known articles in this area.

2 Tencati, A. and Zsolnai, L. (2009). The collaborative enterprise. *Journal of Business Ethics*, 85(3), 367–76 (p. 369).

3 Kuhn, T. (2008). A communicative theory of the firm: developing an alternative perspective on intra-organisational power and stakeholder relationships, *Organisation Studies*, 29(8-9), 1227–54.

4 See, for example, van Riel, C.B.M. and Fombrun, C. (2007). *Essentials of Corporate Communication*. Abingdon: Routledge; Cornelissen, J. (2011). *Corporate Communication*, 3rd edition, London: Sage; Argenti, P. (2008). *Corporate Communication*, New York: McGraw-Hill.

5 Putnam, L.l. and Nicotera, A.M. (2009). *Building Theories of Organisation: The Constitutive Role of Communication*. London: Routledge.

6 Michael Porter's seminal book *Competitive Advantage* published in 1989 by Free Press is the classic on the topic, but the 2008 collection of his essays in *On Competition*, published by *Harvard Business Review*, brings his earlier and more recent thinking together.

7 Although Birger Wernerfelt originated the term 'resource-based view', Jay Barney is recognised as the main proponent of this theory. His often-cited first article is Barney, J. (1991). Firm resources and sustainable competitive advantage, *Journal of Management*, 17(1), 99–120. He can also be seen at www.youtube.com/watch?v=-KN81_oYl1s.

8 Fiol, C.M. (1991). Managing culture as a competitive resource: an identity-based view of sustainable competitive advantage. *Journal of Management*, 17(1), 191–211.

9 Stated by Judge Mervyn King at the World Public Relations Forum, Stockholm, June 2010.

10 Bourdieu, P. (1977). *Outline of a Theory of Practice*. Cambridge and New York: Cambridge University Press.

11 Freeman, R.E. (1984). *Strategic Management: A Stakeholder Approach*. Boston: Pitman.

12 Grunig, J.E. and Hunt, T. (1984). *Managing Public Relations*. New York: Holt, Rinehart & Winston.

13 Maslow, A.H. (1943). A theory of human motivation, *Psychological Review*, 50(4), 370–96.

14 Hallahan, K., Holtzhausen, D., van Ruler, B., Verčič, D. and Sriramesh, K. (2007). Defining strategic communication. *International Journal of Strategic Communication*, 1(1), 3–35.

15 A unified voice, usually in terms of a consistent alignment of all the communicative functions to present a unified corporate identity, is argued by corporate identity and corporate reputation scholars and practitioners such as S. Albert, P.S. Bronn, D. Bernstein, J.M.T. Balmer, C.F. Fombrum, S.A. Greyser, W. Ollins and C.B.M. van Riel.

16 Kuhn, T. (2008). A communicative theory of the firm: developing an alternative perspective on intra-organisational power and stakeholder relationships, *Organisation Studies*, 29(8–9), 1227–54.

17 The enabling and constituting role of communication is much discussed in the communications literature, for example L. Putnam and A. Nicotera above, but also in the public relations literature, for example, Zerfass, A. (2008). Corporate

communication revisited: integrating business strategy and strategic communication. In Zerfass, A., van Ruler, B. and Sriramesh, K. *Public Relations Research. European and International Perspectives and Innovations.* Wiesbaden: VS Verlag Fur Sozialwissenschaften.

3   Leadership and public relations

Introduction

This book conflates ideas around public relations and leadership. Our aim is to bring together a range of insights from both areas to create a usable framework for public relations leaders. However, before we do this it is necessary to separate out these terms and discuss what we mean by public relations and leadership. In Chapter 2 we outline what a public relations view of the world looks like. Here, we set out to define what leadership is and to tease out its most important dimensions for public relations. This discussion serves a number of purposes. First, it highlights that leadership and public relations share many of the same preoccupations. Second, it follows that public relations practitioners should therefore play, and are well suited to, a leadership role in organisations. Finally, the nature of public relations leadership suggests the adoption of particular leadership styles and behaviour.

The chapter is structured under the following headings:

* Where do we start with leadership?
* Diving deeper
* Public relations and leadership come together
* Mind the gap: the need for more research

Where do we start with leadership?

The task of defining leadership is not as easy as might first appear given that it is a pervasive, multi-faceted and contested area of practice. It might even be said that society has become obsessed with the notion of leadership. People talk about its conduct (good, bad or indifferent) in all areas of our social life including business, the military, sport, politics, religion and art. Such discussions highlight the nuances and different dimensions of leadership. For example, the leaders we pass judgement on can hold an official office (Barack Obama) or have no formal position of power (Martin Luther King). They might be regarded as the sole leader to millions of people around the world (Dalai Lama), or one of a few acknowledged leaders in a small team (Spain's magnificent, all-conquering national football squad).

Leadership is also associated with a range of different characteristics and qualities: humility (Mahatma Gandhi), ruthlessness (Rupert Murdoch), glamour (John F. Kennedy), duty (Queen Elizabeth II), iconoclasm (Fidel Castro), fun (Richard Branson) and integrity (Nelson Mandela). The deeds of leaders become individualised and framed as acts of heroism, egotism and selfishness. Are such men and women born or made? What's the secret of their success, or where did it all go wrong? What sort of power and control do they rely on, if any?

These questions highlight that leadership is discussed, conceptualised and defined in many different ways. To help us through this morass Northouse offers a useful marker.[1] He argues that leadership is a *process* through which an individual *influences* a *group* of other individuals to achieve a *common goal*. Those that engage in this process are leaders and the people they lead are their followers. This focus on people serves to clarify a common misconception that arises in organisations about the role of the leader and that of a manager. The two terms are often used interchangeably despite differences existing between the two. For example, a manager is someone who co-ordinates resources and focuses on process and systems, whereas a leader leads and inspires people. This distinction means that a manager can also be a leader. However, just being a manager does not mean you can automatically call yourself a leader[2] – leaders need people to follow them.

Diving deeper

It is worth pausing for a moment to unpack further the thinking behind Northouse's deceptively simple definition. His conceptualisation of leadership as a *process* contradicts the view that it is a trait or characteristic that resides within people.[3] Rather, it is an interactive phenomenon that occurs amongst people – a transaction between the leader and their followers. This idea is important because when leadership is defined in his way 'it becomes available to everyone. It is not restricted to the formally designated leader in a group.'

This dispersed perspective on leadership certainly supports our experience. For example, the real leader in a football team is not always the captain, while an employee may have greater influence over other colleagues on a particular issue than their head of department. Indeed, leaders can be found throughout an organisation rather than just in the executive suite. Leaders are simply people who have followers and formal organisational chart protocol does not always have much to do with this. This is explained in part by the second key concept that is embedded in Northouse's definition.

Influence is the key currency of leaders and they are bankrupt without it. Leadership must involve influence in some shape or form and this can be achieved through the application of different skills or leadership styles. Given the process is situational, leaders need a repertoire to operate in different contexts. Effective leaders change their style to fit the situation. Northouse highlights that leadership is composed of both a directive and supportive dimension and these are applied according to the context.

Leadership also involves more than one person, hence the idea of a *group*. This might be two people sitting in an office (whenever two or more people are gathered together there is the potential for leadership), the local branch of the Women's Institute or the employees of a multi-national company. This reinforces the point made earlier that it is not possible to have leaders without followers. Indeed, if a chief executive cannot influence a group of people in the organisation he or she is experiencing a failure of leadership. This insight leads to the final component of Northouse's definition.

The aim of leadership is to bring people together around a *common goal*. It this idea of mutual endeavour that provides what Northouse calls the 'ethical overtone' of leadership. This highlights the need for leaders to work with their followers to achieve agreed objectives. It highlights the importance of persuasion, cooperation and negotiation. This therefore starts to exclude coercive approaches from the leadership lexicon. Coercion is about one person enforcing their will on another to achieve what they want. It is about force, threats and the raw exercise of power rather than the negotiated pursuit of common goals. Marginalising such approaches is admirable in the abstract but situations do arise in which the leader may not have the time to negotiate and will instead need to impose their will on a situation. A crisis situation is a good example of this. Nevertheless, the idea of common goals serves to highlight that leadership should be less authoritarian and autocratic than previously thought. Rather than being at the top of a pyramid, leaders are encouraged to see themselves at the centre of a circle where their job is to guide, challenge, support and empower.[4] They are inextricably part of a process of influence rather than sitting above it.

This also recognises that essential knowledge and expertise is dispersed throughout the organisation rather than just residing in the heads of senior executives. This challenges the idea that organisational knowledge can be centralised and codified. Rather, it is instead generated by the relationships that exist amongst the employees in an organisation which are characterised by trust and cooperation.[5] This situation therefore requires that it is the knowledge base that should lead the organisation.[6]

Public relations and leadership come together

The increasing focus in leadership studies on participation and involvement complements the emphasis placed in public relations on collaborative decision-making, shared control and relationships[7] (also see Chapter 9 that discusses key behaviours in public relations). Exploratory research has even shown that this complementary way of looking at the world has led, in turn, to a preference in public relations practice towards an inclusive style of leadership.[8] These synergies begin to underline the common ground that exists between a public relations and leadership view of the world. Indeed, these similarities play out in each of the properties of leadership highlighted by Northouse.

First, both public relations and leadership can be regarded as a strategic *process* that enables the organisation to operate effectively. As a process each works within, as well as across, the organisation's departmental functions and external boundaries. They are processes that flow in and around the organisation. Both leaders and public relations practitioners try to avoid seeing the organisation through a single functional lens (see Chapter 2) and operate as boundary spanners connecting themselves with a rich network of stakeholders.

Second, communication is a core competence of public relations and leadership. To *influence* and agree *common goals* requires effective communication throughout the organisation on behalf of leaders. This is why new perspectives in the leadership field highlight that communicative ability is the most important attribute of a leader,[9] particularly during a time of change when followers need to be motivated and inspired.[10] This provides opportunities for public relations. In particular, it highlights how the ability of public relations practitioners to influence others in the organisation is strongly associated with providing vision and acting as a change agent.[11]

This emphasis on vision, change and inspiring others through communication is described as a transformational style of leadership and is seen as especially relevant for public relations.[12, 13, 14] It recognises that the requirement to convert individual self-interest into collective action requires building rapport with colleagues, creating connections and sharing power.[15] This requires leaders being sensitive to the process of decision-making rather than just becoming preoccupied with the generation of a particular outcome.[16] For example, there is no point a leader launching a consultation exercise with employees if a decision has already been taken to pursue a particular course of action.

Working in *groups* requires contextual intelligence and the ability to the see the world from the perspective of others. This capacity is inherent in both public relations and leadership approaches given such awareness is the starting point for building productive relationships with a range of internal and external stakeholders. The intensive social and interactive aspects of leadership and public relations also require each to focus on organisational values. Both need a fully functioning moral compass to ensure their wide ranging engagement activities are governed consistently by the organisation's core values while, from a proactive perspective, values can be used to inspire and engage people. Public relations practitioners and leaders often find themselves as the public face of the organisation during times in which competing issues and priorities collide. A focus on values helps them to do the right thing even when under the most intense pressure.

Mind the gap: the need for more research

The similarities we have just discussed begin to reinforce the progressive leadership role public relations can play in organisations. This is important for an area of practice that has many critics and a well documented image problem.[17] Good public relations leaders are therefore crucial to the future health and prospects of the profession. However, despite the double bonus of opportunity and need, research into public relations leadership is still in its infancy. Few studies have focused on the subject explicitly. Bruce Berger and Bryan Reber are part of a small community of scholars who have sought to plug this gap. Their research has tackled subjects such as influence[18] and the career development of public relations leaders.[19] Elsewhere, others have examined leadership issues such as gender,[20] styles[21] and behaviours.[22] In addition to these recent and specific explorations in public relations, the concept of leadership is implicit in several theoretical perspectives.[23] For example, one of the most comprehensive academic research projects in our area attempted to identify the key characteristics of excellence in public relations practice and set these out as general principles.[24]

Despite a few blooms of inquiry, the canon of leadership research in public relations is still best characterised as a desert sprinkled with the odd oasis rather than a rain forest with a rich and diverse ecology. Of particular concern to us is that there is a big knowledge gap when it comes to understanding the dimensions of leadership in practice.[25] This is a serious shortcoming in a world where public relations practitioners are fighting for organisational legitimacy. New perspectives are required and this book is an attempt to meet this challenge by putting forward a leadership model that has been tested in organisations and developed with practitioners.

Summary

Leadership is an under-researched area in public relations. This is problematic for two reasons that should resonate with both practitioners and academics. First, leadership and public relations are strategic processes that are inextricably linked, rather like the strands of a helix running through the organisation. Second, the public relations profession needs to produce good and effective leaders. Public relations people are well suited to such roles given the synergies that now exist between a leadership and public relations mindset. Leadership is about change and motivating others to work towards agreed objectives while – at the same time – being sensitive to context and the needs of those individuals. It is *people* that leaders need to work with to achieve organisational goals and this is familiar territory for public relations professionals.

This common ground is often framed by a discussion of transformational styles of leadership. This focuses on change, dynamism and action. We end this chapter, however, with the thought that leaders also need to know how and when to relax. Doris Kearns Goodwin is one of the great historians of arguably the highest-profile leadership role on the planet: the American Presidency. One of her biggest fans is Barack Obama and in the year before he became President he revealed that Goodwin's study of Abraham Lincoln[26] is the one book he would take to the White House, apart from the Bible. One of the key conclusions Goodwin has reached about successful leadership after years of scholarship is the importance of being able to switch off and recharge your batteries. Looking back at past Presidents she notes how they were able to ruminate about the day's events: 'These were the days of no television. Leaders weren't worried about cable news or their BlackBerrys. They weren't multi-tasking; they had time to reflect. It's a luxury many leaders just don't have today, and that's a real loss.'[27] Goodwin's perspective from history is important given the point made earlier in the chapter that leadership is situational. There is no fixed, perfect path for leaders. It requires flexibility. Things go wrong, unexpected events happen. Actions result in unanticipated consequences. Books, articles and the advice of others can help, but to navigate through these challenges leaders need to come up for air, reflect, learn lessons, dust themselves off and start again.

Notes

1 Northouse, P.G. (2013). *Leadership: Theory and Practice.* London: Sage. In the sixth edition of his authoritative text Peter Northouse provides an updated, clear and comprehensive overview of the leadership field's major models and theories.
2 For a discussion of the difference between leaders and manager see Bennis's classic account: Bennis, W. (1989). *On Becoming a Leader.* New York: Basic Books.
3 See Jago, A.C. (1982). Leadership: perspectives in theory and research, *Management Science*, 28(3), 315–36.
4 See Smythe, J. (2007). *The Chief Engagement Officer: Turning Hierarchy Upside Down to Drive Performance.* Farnham: Gower.
5 See Stacey, R.D. (2001). *Complex Responsive Processes in Organizations: Learning and Knowledge Creation.* London: Routledge.
6 See Gold, J. (2011). The leader's conundrum or you cannot lift yourself up by your own shirt collar can you? Inaugural lecture, Leeds Business School, Leeds Metropolitan University, 10 February. www.youtube.com/watch?v=J-MF2mJuAVA.
7 Heath, R.L. (2001). Shifting foundations: public relations as relationship building. In Heath, R.L. (ed.), *The SAGE Handbook of Public Relations* (pp. 2–3). Thousand Oaks, CA: Sage.
8 Werder, K.P. and Holtzhausen, D. (2009). An analysis of the influence of public relations department leadership style on public relations strategy use and effectiveness, *Journal of Public Relations Research*, 21(4), 404–27. Werder and Holtzhausen acknowledge the limitations of their study by noting that it measures practitioner perceptions of leadership style rather than actual behaviour.
9 Werder, K.P. and Holtzhausen, D. (2009). An analysis of the influence of public relations department leadership style on public relations strategy use and effectiveness (see above).
10 Eisenberg, E., Goodhall, H.L.J. and Tretheway, A. (2007). *Organisational Communication: Balancing Creativity and Constraint.* Boston, MA: Bedford/St. Martin's.
11 Choi, J. and Choi, Y. (2009). Behavioral dimensions of public relations leadership in organisations, *Journal of Communication Management*, 13(4), 292–309.
12 Werder and Holtzhausen, An analysis of the influence of public relations department leadership style on public relations strategy use and effectiveness.
13 Jin, Y. (2010). Emotional leadership as a key dimension of public relations leadership: a national survey of public relations leaders, *Journal of Public Relations Research*, 22(2), 159–81.
14 Aldoory, L. and Toth, E. (2004). Leadership and gender in public relations: perceived effectiveness of transformation and transactional leadership styles. *Journal of Public Relations Research*, 16(2), 157–83.

15 Aldoory, L. and Toth, E. (2004). Leadership and gender in public relations (see above).

16 Toth, E.L. and Heath, R.L. (eds). (1992). *Rhetorical and Critical Approaches to Public Relations*. Hillsdale, NJ: Lawrence Erlbaum.

17 See L'Etang, J. (2008). *Public Relations: Concepts, Practice and Critique*. London: Sage. This book provides an overview of a range of critical perspectives and how these have been applied to public relations. L'Etang has also edited with Magda Pieczka a volume that brings together a range of prominent critical thinkers: L'Etang, J. and Pieczka, M. (eds) (2006). *Public Relations: Critical Debates and Contemporary Practice*. Mahwah, NJ: Lawrence Erlbaum.

18 Berger, B.K. and Reber, B.H. (2006). *Gaining Influence in Public Relations: The Role of the Resistance in Practice*. Mahwah, NJ: Lawrence Erlbaum.

19 Berger, B.K., Reber, B.H. and Heyman, W.C. (2007). You can't homogenize success in communication management: PR leaders take diverse paths to top, *International Journal of Strategic Communication*, 1(1), 53–71.

20 Aldoory, L. and Toth, E. (2004). Leadership and gender in public relations (see above).

21 See Werder and Holtzhausen, An analysis of the influence of public relations department leadership style on public relations strategy use and effectiveness.

22 Choi, J. and Choi, Y. (2009). Behavioral dimensions of public relations leadership in organisations (see above).

23 Berger, B.K. and Meng, J. (2010). Public relations practitioners and the leadership challenge. In Heath, R.L. (ed.), *The SAGE Handbook of Public Relations* (pp. 421–34). Thousand Oaks, CA: Sage.

24 Grunig, J.E. (ed.) (1992). *Excellence in Public Relations and Communication Management: Contributions to Effective Organizations*. Hillsdale, NJ: Lawrence Erlbaum. Grunig, L.A., Grunig, J. E. and Dozier, D.M. (2002). *Excellent Public Relations and Effective Organizations: A Study of Communication Management in Three Countries*. Mahwah, NJ: Lawrence Erlbaum. Lee, S. and Evatt, D.S. (2005). An empirical comparison of the predictors of excellence in public relations, *Corporate Reputation Review*, 8(1), 31–43.

25 Berger, B.K. and Meng, J. (2010). Public relations practitioners and the leadership challenge (see above).

26 Kearns, D. (2005). *Team of Rivals*: *The Political Genius of Abraham Lincoln*. New York: Simon & Schuster.

27 Coutu, D. (2009). Different voice: leadership lessons from Abraham Lincoln. A conversation with historian Doris Kearns Goodwin. *Harvard Business Review*, 83(4), 43–47, p. 46.

4 Supporting the chief executive

Introduction

A key strategic contribution of public relations in an organisation is supporting and working with the senior-management team. This advisory role requires a close working relationship with one particular individual: the chief executive officer (CEO). Understanding the environment in which the CEO operates is crucial if the public relations leader is to develop a close and productive working relationship with the person who is their most important internal stakeholder. This requires an acute sensitivity to the issues that keep these men and women awake at night and the strategic drivers that shape their world. It also requires a solution-oriented and realistic mindset from the public relations leader to help them rest more easily in their beds.

This chapter therefore seeks to explore some of the contextual challenges confronting chief executives, including key contextual factors as well as how the character of the modern organisation requires a different model of leadership. We argue that these developments not only create a new operating climate for CEOs, but one in which the strategic virtues of public relations have a crucial part to play. These ideas are discussed under the following headings:

* Stakeholder expectations and governance
* Accountability amplified by turbulence and scrutiny
* New leadership challenges in the organisation
* The need for trusted advisers
* Joined in adversity: the CEO and public relations leader
* Situational sensitivity

Stakeholder expectations and governance

The CEO is the one person in the organisation whose boss is not another employee and they are ultimately responsible for results and performance.[1] In contrast to the other executives sitting around the board room table, it is the CEO who ultimately makes the final decisions and tough calls in the organisation. A consequence of this is that they are directly and personally accountable to the organisation's stakeholders. This is a key challenge for chief executives because of the legitimate and growing expectations stakeholders now have of them as individuals and of the organisations[2] they lead.

Implicit in this up-gearing in attitudes is the idea that corporate social responsibility (CSR) is not just about organisations seeking solutions to the social issues generated by their business operations and interests. It is also about a wider duty to act with integrity in their relationships with stakeholders. Indeed, an organisation's overall performance is linked increasingly to how it affects the interests of others in the pursuit of its own interests. If we consider the example of a large retail group the issues the company might generate for 'others' include the pay and conditions of foreign workers in its supply chain or the adverse impact the construction of a new store may have on existing local businesses and residents. While these groups may be further down the stakeholder pecking order than shareholders, customers and employees, their importance is growing and CEOs are judged increasingly on how their organisations behave towards these groups and individuals[3] who are not seen as so crucial to organisational success.

It is also important to recognise that this accountability is covert as well as overt. What we mean by this is that corporate governance in these areas is not just shaped and codified by rules and regulations. These new obligations extend beyond organisations being legally compliant. Rather, it is about how the organisation enacts values based behaviours that other stakeholders regard as fair and appropriate (see Chapter 7). For the CEO governance now means ensuring that decision-making across the organisation aligns with a set of values negotiated with stakeholders (covert accountability), as much as legal and regulatory norms (overt accountability).

Chief executives are grappling with the implication of this new stakeholder driven agenda. Delivering good financial performance and being able to take care of the tangible assets that appear on the organisation's balance sheet is taken for granted. What they are judged on now is their skill in protecting and enhancing the organisation's intangible assets and generating non-financial returns for the organisation. This requires CEOs to recognise that performance is not only measured according to the organisation's self-generated goals, but also by the expectations placed on it by a range of diverse stakeholders. The result of this is that CEOs need to be especially sensitive to the link between values and stakeholder perception.[4]

Accountability amplified by turbulence and scrutiny

For the chief executive this heightened climate of accountability is being conducted within an organisational environment that is characterised by turbulence. Key contributory and destabilising factors are the processes of globalisation and interdependence. Even if an organisation does not operate internationally it can be affected profoundly by developments beyond its national borders. CEOs cannot even be hermetically sealed from events that happen outside of their own sector. Both points are illustrated by the banking crisis of 2008 that is still having a huge impact on businesses of all types, as well as government and organisations from the third sector. Organisations that monitored vigilantly the external environment did not foresee or appreciate the consequences generated by a chain reaction of events caused by bad debt in the North American mortgage market (for a more detailed discussion of this see Chapter 6).

The speed and ubiquity of modern communication technology also ensures that the idea of a little local difficulty is increasingly outdated. For example, we know of the CEO of an international banking group who was discussing the prospects of its Scottish banking subsidiary with a group of financial analysts in Melbourne. He remarked that the Scottish economy had been in recession for 150 years. This was an attempt to provide some colour and context to the challenges the company was facing in this market. The comment was immediately seized on by a journalist 11,000 miles away and became front-page news in the Scottish media. The coverage was particularly damaging for the company's reputation as it sparked a long-running debate that focused on its commitment to its banking brand in Scotland.

Any existing feelings of vulnerability amongst chief executives are intensified by a situation that requires them to communicate with the media more than ever before. This is the arena in which the tensions and debates generated by trying to juggle a diverse set of stakeholder expectations are played out in public. This makes CEOs deeply uneasy. Media scrutiny challenges their decision-making, personal reputation and credibility both within and outside of the organisation. It also highlights the porous boundaries that exist between an organisation's external and internal communication, further underlining the exposure and difficulties that come with communicating simultaneously to many stakeholder groups. For example, the CEO's televised interview will be viewed by customers, service users, suppliers, regulators and politicians, as well as employees.[5]

CEOs are therefore increasingly likely to lose their job due to poor communication skills. The case of Tony Hayward, the former CEO of BP, demonstrates graphically how one throw-away remark in a broadcast interview can spark a chain of events that leads to resignation.[6] Hayward talked of being demonised and vilified in the United States after his infamous 'I'd like my life back' quote following the 2010 oil spill in the Gulf of Mexico.[7] It is this acute level of personal vulnerability that leads Kevin Kelly to conclude that the first preoccupation of the CEO is communication: 'how it can be misunderstood, and how it should be handled'[8] (also see Chapter 3).

Despite communication being regarded as a key competence for chief executives, most receive little formal preparation for the cut and thrust of the media world other than the odd dose of training. Not surprisingly, chief executives look to their senior public relations adviser for guidance and insight in this area.[9] Further, consider that social media has created an additional layer of complexity that again ratchets up a CEO's sense of vulnerability. They are no longer just directly called to account by journalists working for newspapers, radio and television but by a hitherto unknown range of groups and individuals from across the world using a diverse mix of interactive communication platforms.

The changing organisational climate

In addition to the world outside the chief executive's window it is also important to think through the significance of developments inside the organisation and how they impact on what might already start to appear to be an impossible job. Chapter 3 highlighted that the demands placed on leaders are changing. Traditional ways of thinking about how organisations operate are increasingly irrelevant. Gareth Morgan[10] likens the tenets of classical management theory to a metaphor that views the organisation as a machine. This regarded management as a rational, mechanistic process of planning, organisation, command, co-ordination and control. An expectation follows from this that organisations have the potential to operate like machines in a predictable, efficient and reliable manner. In this fairy tale world it was once believed that it might be possible for the CEO to behave like the Wizard of Oz in the famous Hollywood film: out of sight, controlling people and events through a console of wheels and levers, while barking orders into a microphone. Morgan dispels such fanciful notions by highlighting that traditional perspectives on leadership diminish its human aspects and ignore the inconvenient truth that the tasks facing organisations are more complex, uncertain and difficult than those that are performed by most machines.

Contemporary leadership thinking confirms the idea that CEOs need to focus on the social and adaptive aspects of their role. To illustrate the point Tamara Erickson[11] argues that leaders born from 1961 through to 1981 (so-called 'Generation Xers') bring a different mindset to their roles and reject conventional leadership methods. She highlights that what were once thought of as essential leadership skills – setting direction, having the answers, controlling performance, running a tight ship – are less relevant today.

The new organisational context requires an increase in CEOs' collaborative capacity, particularly their ability to create and maintain networks. Rather than focusing on independent decision-making, CEOs must now make room for wide stakeholder participation in order to find answers to the sort of wicked problems modern organisations face. Indeed, we would go so far as to say that one person is not capable of handling all the complexities of the internal and external organisational world, and that building a team with the right capabilities to cover that span of responsibility is essential. Erickson concludes that this realisation inclines CEOs towards establishing and maintaining symmetrical rather than power-based, boss–subordinate relationships. Such a strategic orientation also serves to reinforce the importance of relationships and dialogue within and around the organisation. In particular, there is a growing recognition that organisational knowledge and innovation is the result of complex interactions between networks of stakeholder, including employees.[12] The CEO must set the framework and be a catalyst for such engagement.

The need for trusted advisers

The context we have discussed suggests that the days of the omnipotent CEO 'wizard' at the top of an organisation are numbered. The CEO's job is associated increasingly with inter-personal communication and building relationships. This is why they spend so much time meeting and speaking with colleagues, customers, analysts, partners, officials and competitors. The information and expectations that exist around these relationships frame their decision-making. Indeed, the chief executive can be seen as the organisation's great aggregator. They pull together and synthesise information from a range of sources which they then dissect for strategic clues and cues. It is from this process that patterns and themes emerge which the CEO can start to mould into strategy.[13]

At the heart of this permanent process of learning, however, is a fundamental contradiction for the organisation's decision-maker in chief. The CEO role requires unbiased and credible information. They need to hear the hard truths, as well as a range of different views and objective assessments. Unfortunately, even the senior executives who surround the CEO do not always fulfil this need. They can be guarded, unwilling to raise difficult issues, obsessed with promoting their own agenda, or unable to see the biases inherent in their own arguments.[14]

This information gap is one of the reasons why chief executives need a close relationship with trusted advisers from inside and outside of the organisation. These people help to provide a vital reality check and are an important source of intelligence. For the CEO this advice is largely informal and conversation based. Consequently, advisors do not have to be a member of the board to influence their thinking. Having influence is dependent on being a valuable source of intelligence rather than where a person sits in the organisation's hierarchy. However, it is important to acknowledge that in highly structured, hierarchical organisations gaining direct access to the chief executive can be difficult if an adviser is not formally a member of the senior-executive team. In such situations it is necessary to develop influencing strategies that target those managers who do have the ear of the CEO. This involves shaping insights and intelligence in such a way that it attaches to their agenda. Advisors need to develop a network of connections and understand who their knowledge is important to – and why.

Regardless of where the public relations practitioner resides in the organisation, we would argue that the forces currently shaping the world of organisational leaders requires them to develop a close and direct advisory relationship with their CEO. It is to this common ground that exists between the two roles that we now turn.

Joined in adversity: the CEO and public relations leader

What we have just said might suggest that the public relations leader is ideally placed to be the CEO themselves. That choice is open to them if they are good enough. However, there are fundamental differences between the role of the CEO and the public relations leader. The chief executive has a much wider operational scope (such as around financial performance and human resources), as well as much higher levels of accountability and personal exposure. Nevertheless, the contemporary organisational context that frames the world of the CEO leads them to a strategic space that is familiar territory for public relations practitioners. We would go as far as to argue that the strategic capabilities of the public relations adviser directly support and complement the CEO's key preoccupations. This is not just special pleading on our behalf as passionate advocates of public relations. It is an opinion supported by others from outside of the public relations universe and is nicely illustrated by a short film produced by *Harvard Business Review* which can be found on YouTube.[15] It comprises a series of short interviews with some of the world's leading experts on leadership. Their conclusions serve to outline the role of tomorrow's chief executive. Many of the key qualities that are highlighted mirror the strategic concerns of senior public relations practitioners. These include the importance of engagement, contextual intelligence, connecting with others inside and outside of the organisation, a predisposition towards collaboration and being adept at communicating in a range of mediums (see Chapters 5 and 6).

This common ground is also reinforced by Alan Lafley, the former CEO of Proctor & Gamble, in an article in which he reflects on his career leading one of the world's largest consumer goods companies.[16] Despite entitling the piece *What Only the CEO Can Do* he describes the essence of his job in much the same way a public relations director might conceptualise their own role. He notes, for example, that the specific task of the CEO is to link the external world with the internal organisation. This requires being responsible for understanding it, interpreting it and advocating for it. Only then, according to his analysis, can an organisation operate in a way that enables it to function sustainably. Our own research too with chief executives shows that many have a profound understanding of the importance of communication and regard public relations advice as essential for themselves and their organisations. They also recognise their personal responsibilities to be effective and credible communicators. Given this analysis it is clear why many CEOs now regard themselves as the ultimate guardians of the organisation's reputation,[17] while the context of accountability and turbulence we have just described highlights why they are also acutely aware of the dangerous link that exists between the reputation of the organisation and the person who heads it up.[18]

Situational sensitivity

CEOs that have a very clear picture of this new world devise an organisational game plan in which the public relations leader is a key player. Given the lens through which the public relations leader views the organisation (see Chapter 2) they can work with the chief executive to prioritise the organisations' key stakeholder accountabilities, as well as the strategies for dealing with them. In essence, this is about helping the CEO to think through the implications of a new model of organisational governance.

Fulfilling this role requires the public relations leader to be contextually intelligent not just about the macro forces impacting on the organisation but also about the CEO's own personal situation within the organisation. This micro-climate has the potential to impact on how the CEO approaches their role from a communicative perspective. For example, it is worth considering the climate of expectations surrounding him or her. Were they recruited to save the organisation from extinction? Are they building on the good work of their predecessor? Are they dealing with conflicting expectations, does the senior-management team want to progress with an acquisition while shareholders are calling for stability?

Different situations linked to people, organisational history and expectations can affect the communication style and behaviour of the CEO. While the chief executive may have a natural inclination towards building consensus and listening to others, the weather they face in the organisation may lead them to adopt a more directive and confrontational style. Even more fundamental for the public relations leader is that other issues in the organisation may deflect their attention away from core communicative tasks. In an ailing organisation the energies of the CEO may be focused instead on generating cash, cutting costs or fixing systems.

Summary

The title of chief executive officer resonates with images of power and prestige. These are the men and women in the organisation whose desk is the place where the buck is supposed to stop and where key decisions are signed off. This chapter has shown that a range of macro forces require them to adopt a strategic mindset that should bring public relations into their orbit. Rather than a fleeting collision, the relationship between the CEO and public relations leader should be symbiotic as well as ongoing. Both are required to view the organisation as a holistic entity rather than through a restrictive functional lens. Each should have a clear perspective across the organisation and a strong moral sense of accountability to the world outside. This helicopter view is essential for strategic understanding and for maintaining the organisation's licence to operate. Such a focus leads to a joint preoccupation with reputation, relational capital, values, organisational integrity and good governance.

This common world-view should lead to a situation in which CEOs endorse, enable and participate in a strategic communication process. However, working with the CEO as a trusted adviser requires not just an understanding of the macro issues shaping their world but also an appreciation of the specific situation they operate in. This affinity with the chief executive's world is essential if the public relations leader is to fulfil both their leadership role and strategic potential within the organisation.

Notes

1 Lafley, A.G. (2009). What only the CEO can do, *Harvard Business Review*, May, 54–62.
2 See Arthur W. Page Society (2007). *The Authentic Enterprise*. New York: Arthur W. Page Society. The report can be downloaded from www.awpagesociety.com/images/uploads/2007AuthenticEnterprise.pdf.
3 See Agle, B.R., Mitchell, R.K. and Sonnenfield, J.A. (1999). Who matters to CEOs? An investigation of stakeholder attributes and salience, corporate performance and CEO values, *Academy of Management Journal*, 42(5), 507–25.
4 Agle, B.R., Mitchell, R.K. and Sonnenfield, J.A. (1999). Who matters to CEOs? (see above).
5 For further discussion of this see Welch, M. and Jackson, P.R. (2007). Rethinking internal communication: a stakeholder approach, *Corporate Communication: An International Journal*, 12(2), 177–98.
6 See YouTube/BPCEOTonyHaywardI'dlikemylifeback.
7 See www.telegraph.co.uk/finance/newsbysector/energy/oilandgas/7912338/BPs-Tony-Hayward-resigns-after-being-demonised-and-vilified-in-the-US.html.
8 Kelly, K. (2008). *CEO: The Low Down on the Top Job*. Harlow: FT Prentice Hall.
9 Arthur Page Society (2007). *The Authentic Enterprise*. www.awpagesociety.com/images/uploads/2007AuthenticEnterprise.pdf (downloaded 16 July 2012).
10 Morgan, G. (2006). *Images of Organization*. London: Sage.
11 Erickson, T.J. (2010). The leaders we need now, *Harvard Business Review*, May, 63–66.
12 Clegg, S., Carter, C., Kornberger, M. and Schweitzer, J. (2011). *Strategy: Theory and Practice*. London: Sage.
13 See Mintzberg, H. (2000). *The Rise and Fall of Strategic Planning*. London: Pearson Education. Mintzberg's seminal contribution to management thinking is to make the distinction between deliberate and emergent strategy.
14 David Nadler provides an excellent analysis of the challenges that characterise the CEO's role and what this means for their advisors. See Nadler, D. (2005). Confessions of a trusted counselor. *Harvard Business Review*, 83(9), 68–77.
15 youtube/harvardbusiness/theroleoftomorrowsleaders.
16 Lafley, A.G. (2009). What only the CEO can do. *Harvard Business Review*. May, 54–62.
17 Echo Research (2005). *Maximising Strategic Impact: A Route Map to the Top Table*. A research report for The Communication Directors' Forum, Godalming, Surrey: Echo.
18 White, K. and White, J. (2004). *CEO Views on Reputation Management: A Report on the Value of Public Relations as Perceived by Organisational Leaders*. London: Chime.

5 A new model of strategic public relations

Introduction

In essence the book's Introduction proposed that three factors are crucial to the effective performance of a public relations leader: a thorough understanding of the strategic role that public relations can play within an organisation; an ability to plan strategically; and an awareness of the key competencies and behaviours they need to exhibit in the role. This chapter discusses the first piece of this jigsaw; that is, how can public relations professionals articulate the value and contribution of their role to organisational leaders and other senior colleagues?

The complexity and challenges described in the previous chapters might suggest a role that is incoherent, messy and almost impossible to define. The purpose of this chapter therefore is to provide a practical framework to tackle this. It will also serve as a guide to help professionals work in a strategic and systematic way by providing a structural and diagnostic framework through which they can organise, audit and analyse their current and future activities. Without a clear understanding of what is strategic and what is tactical and an appreciation that strategy operates at different levels, it is impossible to articulate the various roles that public relations can fulfil within an organisation. Furthermore, in the absence of a clear understanding of how different strategic levels relate to and inform each other, there is likely to be confusion about how and when public relations roles change. We have found in our work with senior professionals that they do not always understand these levels, or that a clear understanding of them helps them to adopt a different and appropriate approach. This, in turn, will impact on how tasks are defined and undertaken, and is a major source of support for practitioners as they are then equipped to resist the tendency of some senior managers to define their work tactically rather than strategically.

The framework described in this chapter is a model that we have tested and used extensively in practice. It was originally developed for and is now used throughout the world's fourth largest organisation, the UK National Health Service,[1] and can be applied to the private, public and not-for-profit sectors, which we contend have more in common than they have differences. Indeed, disparities can effectively be reduced to the purpose of the organisation; that is, whether it is shareholders, the public interest or a cause that hold the major stake and which ultimately drive the organisation's orientation. Bearing that in mind, the principles supporting the model are deliberately designed to be generic and applicable to any kind of organisation, the model also accommodates the fact that the neat dividing lines that once characterised organisational life are no longer relevant in practice, Indeed, some organisations serve multiple purposes and occupy a hazy middle ground. For example, a state-funded hospital that seeks to serve the public interest may also be required to compete for specialist services and patients, or a listed company may enact values in actions which genuinely serve wider societal interests.

This chapter looks at the strategic role of public relations leaders under four headings:

* Roles in general
* The four-by-four model
* The contribution of public relations at four strategic levels
* The four attributes: DNA strands

Roles in general

Before going into detail about the strategic model that forms the heart of this chapter (as well as the book itself), it is important to clarify the word 'role'. Practitioners often talk about the role they play within their organisation and the succeeding paragraphs of this chapter talk about the 'roles' that public relations can play at different levels of organisational strategy.

The notion of roles emanates from role theory which is a concept drawn from sociology. Role theory contends that much of everyday life involves individuals spending time in groups and acting out a variety of positions or roles within them, for example as mother within a family group, as social club secretary in a social group, as accountant within a company, as manager within a department and so on. People take cues from those around them and learn to adapt behaviours depending on the positions they occupy. In other words, the role and consequently the tasks allocated to the role are profoundly influenced by the expectations of others. Over time these expectations become norms that then define the role. A key principle is that organisations, mainly their senior managers, define roles depending on their perceptions of what they should be. Hence, if senior managers have a limited or skewed perception of what public relations can contribute, then it is likely that public relations will find itself limited to that role. A task for public relations may therefore be to expand the role by educating and demonstrating to management that it can contribute to organisational effectiveness by fulfilling a more comprehensive and strategic remit.

There have been several attempts in the public relations literature to define the role of public relations, most notably by Broom and Smith[2] and then by Dozier and Broom,[3] who proposed that there were two basic public relations roles. Simply put, these roles were *communication manager*, who is involved in policy making and planning, and *technician*, who is involved in implementing programmes. Since this early work, there has been considerable writing on public relations roles,[4] but suffice to say that the model put forward in this chapter will generate a number of roles for the practitioner, which the authors believe encapsulate and extend previous work.

One final point to make about roles which again will serve to clarify some confusion. Roles can be constructed in two ways. First, there is the role the whole public relations department fulfils and that will be determined by the expectations that the organisation has of the function as a whole. Second, the department itself will comprise individuals with different knowledge, skills and expertise sets and who themselves fulfil different roles both within the team and within the organisation. Hence the role of the most senior public relations professional will be quite different from that of the most junior: our focus here is on the role of the most senior practitioner.

The four-by-four model

There is a huge amount on the contribution public relations makes to organisational effectiveness in the academic literature. Our view is that Steyn's[5] study, using a strategic-management perspective, mapping the contribution of communication at various levels of business operation (enterprise, corporate, business unit, functional and operational), is a useful starting point. However, Steyn's work focuses exclusively on the private sector where the minority of practitioners work. Nevertheless, it has the potential to be further contextualised and adapted for practice.

Having worked extensively with both the private, public and not-for-profit sectors, the authors have devised an alternative model for the contribution of public relations. It is called the four-by-four model and consists of the elements shown in Figure 5.1: the four elements in the pyramid represent the organisation, split into the different levels at which it operates. The outer ring represents the various stakeholder communities on which it depends, but this should be regarded as a constantly dynamic network permeating and embracing the four organisational elements, rather than as a separate variable. Stakeholders are shown as a network because organisations have several, are ultimately dependent on them and are held in a web of relationships with and by them, whether they be internal or external to the organisation. As Starck and Kruckeberg have said, 'Corporations ultimately operate by consent of society, which remains in fact the ultimate stakeholder'.[6] They are also shown as a network because the reality is that organisations are pulled towards different stakeholders at different times and with different intensity. For example, in the aftermath of the global financial crisis banks were pulled closer to regulatory and governmental stakeholders as those bodies sought to exert greater power in response to the crisis in the banking sector. Furthermore, the network is of course interconnected itself. The

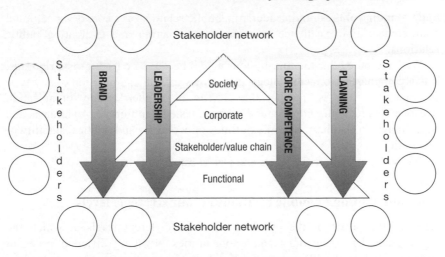

Figure 5.1 The four-by-four model of strategic public relations

stakeholder network has a tension, rather like a spider's web, with the organisation seeking equilibrium between the competing demands of a range of stakeholders.

Organisations are complex and the stakeholder environment in which they operate is dynamic. Many metaphors can be used to describe the stakeholder environment. One favoured by us takes the sea as its inspiration and highlights the importance of meteorological and navigation skills for the public relations leader, that is, an ability to analyse and predict external conditions, as well as the ability to guide an organisation past both visible and 'hidden' dangers. It also highlights the importance of insight which allows the organisation to work with the prevailing conditions for maximum effect. Indeed, the stakeholder environment can be with the organisation and it can glide along with the tide, while at other times forces can combine to create a treacherous environment that can threaten its very existence.

The model attempts to make sense of this context by examining the organisation at different strategic levels: societal, corporate, value chain and functional. The model recognises that an organisation is a nexus of connections between stakeholders who not only fall into one or more of the organisational stakeholder categories identified in the four levels, but also that the levels and therefore stakeholders are interconnected. The stakeholders ultimately determine and define the nature of an organisation, providing its licence to operate and without whose cooperation it will cease to exist. The framing of the model in this way also recognises that a stakeholder may have multiple relationships with the organisation and will interact differently depending on that context.

Our research for this model also identified four distinct attributes, which we describe as DNA strands. These strands characterise leading public relations at whatever level it is being undertaken. They are: an excellent understanding of the brand; leadership; public relations as a core organisational competence; and excellence in planning, managing and evaluating public relations.

We have called this the four-by-four model because we find it to be rigorous: it is a comprehensive methodology that allows careful examination of any type of organisation. It is transportable: it can be applied to any organisation irrespective of country context, and we have tested it in Europe, Australasia and Scandinavia. It is robust: it works in times of economic and political stability or instability.

We will now explore the levels and DNA strands in more detail.

The contribution of public relations at four strategic levels

Each of the layers of the pyramid represent different levels at which the organisation has obligations and opportunities involving different types of decision-making and different types of stakeholders.

Societal level

At the societal level, an organisation seeks to obtain legitimacy for itself by trying to gain and maintain overall support from society as a whole. Its place, standing and reputation in society determine whether its 'licence to operate' is granted and supported by public opinion. Here the values (see Chapter 7 for more on values) on which the organisation is based are tested and are either found true or found wanting. Its purpose and direction are also put to the same test.

Public relations should play a central role in helping to clarify the organisation's values and mission, as well as monitoring the way it goes about achieving those to determine whether they are acceptable to society generally. The organisation's reputation – that is, the associations people carry around in their heads about a particular company, public-sector body or cause – with the general public is an indicator of current societal approval or, indeed, disapproval. The public relation's function, then, acts as the organisational antennae by undertaking the boundary-spanning role indicated earlier in this book: constantly monitoring the external environment and public opinion, to bring essential intelligence into the organisation so that its management can act accordingly. The public relations function collects evidence about and makes judgements on how society perceives the organisation and identifies any action that may be required if there are issues to be addressed. It also promotes the organisation by the clear communication of its values and purpose and demonstrating consistency of performance against them.

As is discussed in greater detail in Chapter 6 this role requires high levels of contextual intelligence as the public relations practitioner helps the organisation's leaders to make sense of an external environment that is in a permanent state of flux.

Corporate level

At the corporate level, organisations largely focus on financial and business goals. This is the level at which the resources of the organisation are marshalled and the precise scope and nature of the organisation is framed so that it can achieve its mission. Here hard questions are asked because this is where choices have to be made. Even in times of organisational plenty, resources have to be used wisely and effectively for it to maintain societal and stakeholder approval and to ensure it is operating effectively and efficiently. Apart from the more obvious resources that have to be in place such as financial, human, technological, estate and so on, as Laurati argues, the cognitive and behavioural resources of the organisation also have to be secured to ensure success.[7] There are three elements to this.

First, the organisation has to ask if it has the reputation it needs in order to achieve what it aspires to do. For example, a local company with a reputation for ignoring local community concerns will not be believed if it wants to position itself as an exemplar of social responsibility. It will have to build local reputational capital in community responsibility first, or it could well find itself exposed to ridicule and opposition.

Second, the organisation will need to ensure it has the relationships that it needs to achieve its objectives. For example, a hospital may have a good reputation, but unless it has spent time building relationships with the organisations that fund and commission its services, it will not be able to gain the necessary support for the changes it feels it should make to the services it delivers.

Third, unless the culture of the organisation internally is aligned to what it wishes to promote externally, again it will not succeed. For example, if a company is presenting itself as customer-friendly and the experience of those contacting the organisation is that staff are slow and generally unhelpful, then it will lose all credibility. It will need to ensure staff are trained and 'bought-in' culturally to the customer-service ethos before it attempts to promote this value externally.

Arguing a case based on what reputational, relational and cultural resources are required for the organisation to succeed positions the public relations function in quite a different place: as a corporate-level discipline and peer with other disciplines recognised as having corporate significance. This kind of approach is very different from asking for resources to mount an online campaign aimed at the local community, which will be a purely tactical discussion. It could well be that to build the reputational and relational capital needed for an organisation to meet its objectives requires an online campaign aimed at the local community, but the starting point for the discussion is entirely different: it is corporate and strategic, not operational and tactical. Using the language and disciplines of business at corporate level is important. The HR director will argue for the human assets required to deliver the organisational vision and the business unit director will make a case for their operational area in similar terms. Public relations should be no exception.

As well as presenting the case for public relations being a strategic asset, the public relations area can make another critical contribution at corporate level. It can support management in making enlightened decisions by ensuring that multiple-stakeholder perspectives are taken into account when resource decisions are made. So, for example, shareholders are a very important stakeholder group, but if their interests are put before all other stakeholders' legitimate claims, the organisation will create issues for itself. The interest of all stakeholders must be properly balanced within the declared value base. So, for example, if an organisational value is to protect the interests of the most disadvantaged, then the needs of that group must be properly accommodated in resource allocation even in difficult times and they should not be left with whatever is left when all other and perhaps more powerful stakeholder needs have been considered. It is the job of the public relations function to ensure these less powerful interests are represented and that all stakeholder interests are balanced. It is at this level where the organisational values which are espoused internally and externally are tested and the public relations function is a guardian of those values and their continued enactment.

It is also the task of the public relations professional to provide intelligence on how the organisation's corporate decisions are likely to be perceived by stakeholders and, of course, to involve stakeholders in, and inform them of, corporate-level decisions as appropriate. Stakeholder involvement can have a profound impact on the nature and scope of the business and its facilitation is a strategic contribution by public relations. Harley Davidson, for example, involve their Harley Davidson Owners' Group (HOG) in discussions about the nature of the business and this guides management decision-making.

Finally, as indicated earlier, it is neither desirable nor possible for the public relations function to be totally responsible for all the organisation's relationship-building and communication activity. An essential role of the senior public relations professional at corporate level is to coach and mentor other senior managers in communicating the organisation's objectives and decisions to their peers and stakeholder groups, and ensuring that they too are alert to the reputational and relational opportunities and threats inherent in doing so.

Value-chain level

At the value-chain level, the focus will be on those stakeholders directly involved in, and with the organisation. Their closeness to the organisation distinguishes them from the broad societal level stakeholders, often called the 'general public', who may have no specific or strong link with it but who form the substance of those norms that form public opinion and who will hold the organisation to account accordingly. Typical value-chain stakeholders will include customers, service users, delivery partners, suppliers, distributors, regulators, employees, and so on. It is at this value-chain stakeholder level that societal and corporate intentions and decisions are made real by being operationalised. The public relations function has a part to play in engaging with these 'close' stakeholders, including those who may be regarded as troublesome, such as activist groups and online communities. This engagement could be for a range of reasons: to involve them in decision-making, to keep them informed, to persuade them to buy or to sell, to identify and work through their current and future concerns, to identify potential issues and crises, to capitalise on opportunities they raise, to solve common problems, and so on. Specific expertise in stakeholder identification, segmentation, insight, engagement and collaboration and/or management can be offered by the public relations department alongside coaching and mentoring those colleagues who interact with these stakeholders regularly. In addition, the public relations function can offer help in detecting, balancing and managing what could well be the conflicting demands of different stakeholder groups and navigating complex negotiations and relationships between them and management.

A very specific and important skill is the insight that public relations professionals can provide on specific groups of stakeholders and individuals. This will be covered in greater detail in Chapter 10, but knowing stakeholders intimately, being able to judge how they are likely to behave and how that behaviour can be influenced is a critical skill of practitioners.

As indicated earlier, being alert to the differences between internal culture and behaviours and external expectations of that culture and behaviour is especially important at this level. Individuals are representatives of the organisation and the brand, and how they behave and communicate will affect the reputation of the whole organisation. This is precisely why so much attention is now being paid to the internal stakeholder, with communication being central to successful cultural and organisational change.

The role of the public relations function in being attuned to and representing all these 'close' stakeholder perspectives, internal and external, to senior managers in the organisation is critical to organisational success.

Functional level

At the functional level, it is the role of public relations to liaise with the other specialist functional areas of the organisation to determine how the functional department called public relations as a whole can contribute its specific communication skills to the organisation's mission and objectives at an operational level. For public relations this will involve planning specific programmes and campaigns which support these objectives, offering specialist public relations advice and services to other functional areas of the organisation in support of their objectives, and coaching and mentoring colleagues throughout the organisation to be 'communicatively competent', or at least communicatively aware, so that they can either undertake certain public relations tasks themselves to an adequate standard, or be clear about when they need to enlist the help of the specialists. The types of specific activities the public relations function will be involved in commonly include (but this is not the complete list):

- constructing communication programmes and activities to support delivery of organisational priorities;
- advising management and delivering campaigns of different types depending on the requirements of the stakeholder group involved, for example social-marketing programmes for behaviour change (e.g. childhood obesity), mass-media campaigns for information dissemination (e.g. new online services to support more traditional retail services), personalised/one-to-one engagement (e.g. with regulators or key delivery partners);
- using recognised business disciplines to design effective communication plans which also embrace the full range of communication techniques, including social marketing and online;
- moving seamlessly between reactive, proactive and interactive roles depending on the relationship with the stakeholder involved;
- evaluating programmes and communication activities for effectiveness.

At this level, a great deal of time is spent on putting together public relations plans of different types depending on the needs of the stakeholder groups involved. Hence, social-marketing programmes may be needed to encourage behavioural change in society as a whole, for example adopting healthy lifestyles; marketing campaigns will be aimed at potential customers to help product sales; lobbying campaigns targeted at MPs individually will be mounted to influence voting intentions; and so on.

Each plan will be different depending on its purpose, who is involved, their communication channel-use habits, the timing of the campaign, and so on. However, the disciplines behind the planning process are the same and Chapter 10 covers the bases on this.

The point of going through the strategic levels at which public relations can make a contribution is to:

- generate a better understanding of organisational strategy and how this might be conceptualised for PR practitioners;
- clarify the types of input that public relations can make to the organisation as a whole, including its input to organisational decision-making;
- demonstrate that public relations contributes more to an organisation than just programmes and campaigns – it can make a strategic input at all levels;
- show that programmes and campaigns have to be seen within a broader context and ensure all programmes are aligned to societal, corporate and/or stakeholder objectives;
- enable the practitioner to articulate and move between the various roles that they must play within the organisation.

The four attributes: DNA strands

Having looked at the four levels of strategic accountability where communication can make a significant contribution, it is now appropriate to examine the four attributes that characterise good communication.

An excellent understanding of the brand

Brands often operate at two levels which we will call background and foreground brands. There are some brands that are internationally known such as Singapore Airlines, Apple, Pepsi-Cola, McKinsey & Co, Toyota, AstraZeneca and the US Army. The 'general public' will have a perception of those brands, even though they may never have experienced them. Much of that perception will be coloured by the industry sector it operates in, the country in which it is headquartered and the public opinion that prevails about it. These brands are very powerful and intersect with and shape our lives and society. Some private-sector brands such as Google and Coca-Cola are financially larger than many country economies and it is salutary to reflect that modern life would be very different without powerful search engines. Foreground brands are those that are personally experienced and to which there is more or less emotional or utilitarian attachment. Background and foreground brands can be combined. A good example is the UK NHS. The service and the values it seeks to represent are a virtual proxy for British values as a whole: respect, fairness, compassion for those unable to help themselves and embodying an ideal held since the inception of the NHS in 1948, that good healthcare should be available to all, regardless of wealth.[8] There is a strong emotional attachment between British people and the NHS; indeed a former Chancellor of the Exchequer, Nigel Lawson, stated that the NHS is 'the nearest thing the UK has to a national religion'.[9] It is a source of national pride and the British people have a strong sense that it is theirs – they own it and are connected with it literally from cradle to grave. It is associated with matters of essential importance and with key rites of passage such as birth, parenthood and death. Against this national background and sentiment, it is at the local level that most people experience the NHS through visits to their family doctors and local hospitals. The national and the local are, however, indivisible and the brand concept has to take this into account.

The concepts of brands and branding are enormously complex.[10] We would contend that the NHS is among the most complex brands. The NHS's simple white logotype on a solid light-blue rectangular background is instantly recognised by 98 per cent of the UK's population[11] and evokes a deep and complex response. The essence of the brand is defined in the NHS Constitution,[12] which describes its purpose, principles and values alongside the rights and responsibilities that drive it.

A deep understanding of that brand and what it means to the wide range of stakeholders who associate with it and believe they own it is essential for communicators to undertake their role effectively. Their task is to demonstrate how NHS brand values are brought to life by NHS organisations in their words and actions and to ensure that stakeholder views are taken into account when developing the brand locally.[13] It is more than simply communicating messages: it is an exchange between staff, service users and the wider community to ensure that the NHS brand 'lives' the values it propounds. The role of the communicator is to act as brand guardian and champion, and to act as a catalyst for change if the reality of the brand experienced is different from the brand espoused.

Leadership

It is apparent that in order for the public relations leader to act across the four levels outlined above and to undertake the roles required as specified across the four attributes, they will require organisational power and need to exercise strong leadership. This is discussed in detail in Chapter 3 on leadership and Chapter 11 on the organisational catalyst. Their place in the organisation is politically and practically important and where they are placed is a clear indicator of whether management recognises that communication is far more than the deployment of a set of communication skills and techniques. According to the Chief Executive of the National Health Service,[14] communication is a core systems asset concerned with building the reputational and relationship capital of the NHS in order to promote, protect and deliver the health of the nation.

Public relations as a core organisational competence

Given the arguments articulated earlier in this chapter that public relations leaders should be engaged in equipping others with public relations skills at all levels, it is clear that responsibility for good communication does not rest on the public relations function alone. It is the responsibility not only of all managers, but all staff, in much the same way as good budgetary discipline is not just the responsibility of the finance function. Staff throughout organisations engage with customers and other stakeholders and to stakeholders staff are the embodiment of the brand.[15] In conceptualising what 'Good in Public Relations' looks like, therefore, it is important for the communication function to recognise the contribution of non-specialist colleagues. The role of the public relations professional is to work with senior management on employee engagement recognising that the clearer and more engaged staff are in developing the organisation's vision and narrative,[16] and the more they are active advocates and intelligence gatherers, the greater the communicative and reputational impact.

Excellence in planning, managing and evaluating public relations

The fourth DNA strand concerns how the department or individuals formally charged with public relations (the function) undertakes its programmes and campaigns. These can be reactive, that is responding to threats and opportunities such as those sometimes posed by the media; proactive, that is implementing planned communication strategies; and/or interactive, that is engaging in dialogue through face-to-face, digital and other channels.

There are a number of well-used planning models for communication which have found wide acceptance in the practitioner community, for example those by Broom[17] and Gregory.[18] These are based recognisably on business planning models.[19] These communication planning models emphasise the importance of research, defining objectives, identifying stakeholders, developing a strategy, selecting appropriate channels, crafting suitable content, identifying issues and risks, deciding on the resources needed and monitoring and evaluating programmes and campaigns. By managing and evaluating programmes with recognised business discipline and in an effective and efficient way, the communication function gains credibility and can demonstrate its contribution to the organisation (for more on this see Chapter 10).

Summary: the four principal roles

The four levels and four attributes together are intended to achieve a number of objectives. First to improve trust, re-enforce legitimacy and to build and defend reputation. Second, by bringing understanding of the broader societal context and the stakeholder perspective into organisations it seeks to facilitate informed decision-making at all levels. Third, to ensure that senior managers as a whole are better equipped to understand the role of public relations in building good, supportive stakeholder networks and to be a part of that skilled cadre themselves. Fourth, to ensure organisational structure, systems and processes (see Chapter 11 on the organisational catalyst) and what they offer are designed and delivered in accordance with the spirit of the brand, and that those in their value chain are

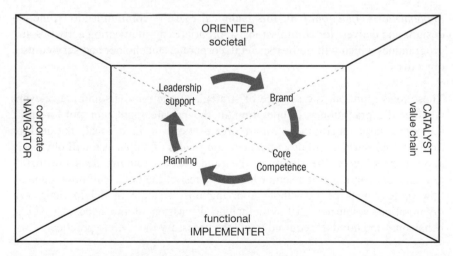

Figure 5.2 A conceptualisation of the four levels of the public relations function with the four permeating attributes

informed and supported by public relations. Finally, that the public relations contributes fully and appropriately at all levels of the organisation. As Sir David Nicholson, former Chief Executive of the NHS, stated: 'In future I expect senior leaders and senior professional communicators to make the communication process an integral part of their institution, so that every organisation within the NHS becomes a "communicating organisation".'[20]

In conclusion, we propose that the strategic public relations leader undertakes four roles within the organisation:

Orienter – societal: The communicator as protector of the organisation, ensuring that the licence to operate and its societal mandate is maintained by keeping the system orientated in the direction that maintains stakeholder support. Articulation and living the brand values is critical and communication has an essential role to play by informing, involving and engaging with societal-level stakeholders to maintain the legitimacy of the brand.

Navigator – corporate: Ensuring that stakeholder perspectives are brought into resource decision-making, ensuring that relational and reputational capital and cultural alignment is factored in as a key resource and integral to the organisation navigating a way through conflicting stakeholder demands is a key role.

Catalyst – value chain: Embedding a value chain, stakeholder perspective in the design, creation and delivery of products and services requires the communication function to provide vision-critical intelligence, engagement capability and evaluation to ensure the delivery of organisational objectives. Here the function is as catalyst for the organisation ensuring values are lived and changing realities rather than changing perceptions.

Implementer – functional: In this technical role the communication function designs and delivers (or commissions) appropriate communication activities and programmes which will deliver societal, corporate, stakeholder and service-user objectives.

These roles represent the essence of strategic public relations and are relevant whether the practitioner is operating in the private, public or not-for-profit sectors; a large, medium or small organisation; or in a local, national or international setting. Although nuances and shades of emphasise will obviously apply depending on the situation, the fundamentals remain the same for all practitioners operating at a senior level. The rest of the book will now focus on how professionals can go about applying this strategic model in their own organisation, a journey that will include discussion of the necessary skills, behaviours and mindset required to put the necessary theory into practice.

Notes

1 See the NHS guidance document NHS (2009). *The Communicating Organisation: Using Communication to Support the Development of High-performing Organisations.* London: NHS. Available at www.dh.gov.uk/prod_consum_dh/groups/dh_digitalassets/documents/digitalasset/dh_110342.pdf.

2 Broom, G.M. and Smith, G.D. (1979). Testing the practitioner's impact on clients, *Public Relations Review*, 5(3), 47–59.

3 Dozier, D.M. and Broom, G.M. (1995). Evolution of the manager role in public relations practice. *Journal of Public Relations Research*, 7(1) 3–26.

4 See, for example, the work of Steyn in Steyn, B. (2009). The strategic role of public relations is strategic reflection: a South African research stream. *American Behavioral Scientist*, 53(4), 516–32, and Moss and colleagues, DeSanto, B. and Moss, D.A. (2004). Rediscovering what PR managers do: rethinking the measurement of managerial behavior in the public relations context, *Journal of Communication Management*, 9(2), 179–96; Moss, D.A. and Green, R. (2001). Re-examining the manager's role in public relations: what management and public relations research teaches us, *Journal of Communications Management*, 6(2), 118–32; Moss, D.A., Newman, A. and DeSanto, B. (2005). What do communications managers do? Defining and refining the core elements of management in a public relations/communication context. *Journalism and Mass Communication Quarterly*, 82, 873–90; Moss, D.A., Warnaby, G. and Newman, A. (2000). Public relations practitioner role enactment at the senior management level within UK companies, *Journal of Public Relations Research*, 12(4), 277–307.

5 Steyn, B. (2007). Contribution of public relations to organisational strategy formulation. In Toth, E.L. (ed.) *The Future of Excellence in Public Relations and Communication Management.* Mahwah, NJ: Lawrence Erlbaum Associates.

6 Starck, K. and Kruckeberg, D. (2001). Public relations and community: a reconstructed theory revisited. In Heath, R.L. (ed.), *The Sage Handbook of Public Relations*, Thousand Oaks, CA: Sage.

7 Laurati, F. (2008). Institutionalising Public Relations. Plenary Panel, European Public Relations Education and Research Association, Milan, October.

8 NHS (2012). About the NHS: Overview. Retrieved 29 May 2012 from www.nhs.uk/NHSEngland/thenhs/about/Pages/overview.aspx.

9 Lawson, N. (1992). *The View from No. 11: Memoirs of a Tory Radical.* London: Bantam Press

10 For more information about brand complexity see Brakus, J.J., Schmitt, B.H. and Zarantonello, L. (2009). Brand experience: what is it? How is it measured? Does it affect loyalty? *Journal of Marketing*, 73, 52–68 and de Chernatony, L. (2009). Towards the holy grail of defining 'brand'. *Marketing Theory*, 9, 101–5.

11 NHS (2012). About the NHS: Overview (see above).

12 The NHS Constitution for England (2012 Edition) can be found at www.dh.gov.uk/prod_consum_dh/groups/dh_digitalassets/@dh/@en/documents/digitalasset/dh_132958.pdf.

13 Gregory, A. (2007). Involving stakeholders in developing corporate brands, *Journal of Marketing Management*, 23(1–2), 59–73.

14 NHS (2009) The communicating organisation: using communication to support the development of high-performing organisations. London: NHS. Available at www.dh.gov.uk/prod_consum_dh/groups/dh_digitalassets/documents/digitalasset/dh_110342.pdf.

15 For more on staff as brand representatives see Maxwell, R. and Knox, S. (2009). Motivating employees to 'live the brand': a comparative case study of employer brand attractiveness within the firm. *Journal of Marketing Management*, 25, 893–907 and Smythe, J. (2007). *The CEO: Chief Engagement Officer.* Aldershot: Gower.

16 Gregory, A. (2007). Involving stakeholders in developing corporate brands (see above).
17 Broom G.M. (2008). *Cutlip and Center's Effective Public Relations* (10th edition), Upper Saddle River, NJ: Prentice Hall International.
18 Gregory, A. (2010). *Planning and Managing Public Relations Campaigns*. London: Kogan Page.
19 As summarised, for example, by Johnson, G., Scholes, K. and Whittingham, R. (2008) *Exploring Corporate Strategy* (8th edition) London: Pearson Education.
20 NHS (2009). The communicating organisation, p. 2 (see above).

Part II

The preoccupations of public relations leaders

Having looked at the strategic contribution of public relations and public relations leadership in its broadest sense, we now turn to the preoccupations of those practitioners who operate at the highest levels. Our work with and observations of public relations leaders has shown us that these four preoccupations are the permanent backcloth to all their work. They are constant and recurring touchstones which provide the focus and compass of their professional lives.

The first is contextual intelligence. Public relations leaders are massively sensitive to what is going on both outside and inside the organisation: they are the organisational antennae, constantly enquiring, sensing, interpreting and articulating what is going on and what may happen. We have found that chief executives find this one of the most valuable contributions that their public relations leaders make. They rely on them for the reality check and for the intelligence they bring on opportunities and potential threats.

The second preoccupation is around organisational values. The public relations leader is uniquely placed to work with senior executives on determining and testing those values and to hold the organisation to account to those values by ensuring that decisions reflect them and behaviours enact them. Values encapsulate the character and heart of an organisation and are therefore deeply bound up with issues of trust and reputation. This is public relations territory and the senior practitioner guards it closely.

The twin of values is organisational ethics. Very few practitioners have had any formal ethical training, yet being able to explain the ethical basis on which they make recommendations and decisions so that they can be consistent and accountable is vital for personal and organisational standing and integrity. Public relations leaders have a strong ethical core, can articulate it clearly and apply it as a matter of course.

The fourth preoccupation is on enacting the role of the public relations leader. Again, we have found that senior practitioners know that certain behaviours are required if they are to be taken seriously. Skills and knowledge are of course vitally important and necessary, but on their own they are not sufficient. Astute public relations leaders are aware that their behaviours, or competencies, help to determine the role that they will be given in their organisation. They are acute observers of organisational culture and understand precisely what is required to gain the respect of senior leadership. Our research has identified a number of key competencies that are demonstrated by the most senior public relations leaders.

6 Contextual intelligence

Introduction

Understanding the context in which the organisation operates is a defining characteristic of public relations leadership in each of the strategic levels described in Chapter 5. It is about being sensitive to the expectations others place on the organisation, spotting threats and opportunities, and generating insights and connections that enhance stakeholder relationships, as well as communicating in a way that is in tune with the times. This strategic obsession with context, forward intelligence and understanding others is the reason why chief executives prize public relations advice (see Chapter 4). It is a vital input to their own process of ongoing, strategic deliberation.

This chapter explores the concept of contextual intelligence and shines a light on a number of important issues relevant to the public relations leader:

- What is contextual intelligence?
- Having the right strategic mindset
- Tackling big picture challenges
- Focusing on your value chain and generating actionable insight

What is contextual intelligence?

Contextual intelligence is an important theme in other chapters and runs like a strand of DNA through this book. It is a vital diagnostic skill for all organisational leaders, as well as being a central tenet of strategic public relations practice. Organising and managing always occurs in a specific context. This frames the attitudes and actions of stakeholders towards particular policies, events and communication. It is also the place from which threats and opportunities emerge.

Trying to make sense of the world and its impact upon us is a key human faculty. Robert Sternberg,[1] the distinguished American psychologist, generally equates intelligence to how well an individual deals with the environmental challenges they encounter during their life. Furthermore, his three components of contextual intelligence have particular resonance for organisations as well as for individuals:

- the ability to adapt to the context you are in by changing something in yourself;
- the ability to change the context you are in to create a better fit between you and it;
- the capacity to recognise when it is time to move out of one context into a more rewarding one.

This process of adaptation and change is the reason good leaders look out from the organisation in an attempt to understand a fluid, dynamic and unpredictable external environment. It is difficult for organisations to be successful over time and to survive they must flex and bend to the vicissitudes of the external environment. This is why environmental analysis is usually the first stage of strategy formulation (see Chapter 10). Indeed, strategy is essentially the process that seeks to ensure the best fit between an organisation and its external environment.[2] Making strategy is, however, a fluid and dynamic process. An executive team may consciously develop a strategy based on the information they have available to them at a given point of time but as the organisation interacts with its environment this will need to change as issues emerge.[3]

Having the right strategic mindset

The reason the strategy process is messy is that understanding the external environment is not a clear-cut process derived from precise questions and answers. The world outside our window is the territory of fuzzy issues:[4] we can never be sure about the actions of stakeholders, the direction of public policy, the longevity of popular trends, the importance of particular developments in our sector, or the impact of new technology. This situation serves to create a permanent climate of uncertainty around the organisation. This means being in a position of having limited knowledge, unable to describe the future and/or faced with the situation where there may be more than one outcome.[5] For public relations practitioners analysing this landscape is the time in their working lives where they occupy vulnerable, 'not knowing' or 'not knowing with much confidence' spaces.

We will see later in the chapter that developing capacity and capability in the field of contextual intelligence involves formal planning, process and an attempt at rational analysis. However, to only rely on such processes misses the point about the context we have just described. The complexity of this environment significantly reduces an organisation's ability to predict and interpret what is going on. The interactions between a huge number of different phenomena – social, psychological, political, cultural, physical and economic – creates a combustible cocktail that generates multiple chains of reaction that it is impossible to anticipate and understand. This means that even small events can have a disproportionately large impact that defies rational analysis at the time.[6] To illustrate the point consider how an undergraduate student working in his bedroom in 2004 launched an electronic social network that has since transformed personal and organisational communication around the world. Mark Zuckerberg is now worth billions of dollars and Facebook is a powerful global brand.

This discussion is designed to serve two purposes. First, it should provide a warning against feelings of omnipotence by the public relations leader: the organisational environment is plagued by uncertainty. Second, it highlights the need to develop a mindset that emphasises flexibility and alertness over pre-planned or standardised responses to environmental developments.[7] The leader's sense making process needs to be nourished as much by personal, improvised and ad hoc information channels as it is by formal organisational systems associated with environmental scanning, data analysis and trend spotting.[8] This means that public relations leaders have to develop their own networks of dissident information to supplement and challenge these official channels. This might involve cultivating relationships with think tanks, universities and pressure groups to provide alternative views on the key issues that are affecting the organisation's environment. Leadership in this context requires perspective and this is best achieved through talking with people who can provide a range of different vantage points. In a situation characterised by vague questions and muddy answers the best strategy is engaging with others and connecting to their networks.

Tackling big-picture challenges

Keeping in mind the health warning about strategic mindset, how should public relations practitioners start to go about making sense of the world? How can they begin to identify the trends that will have the biggest operational impact? What are the most important issues that affect the organisation? Trying to address these questions is an ongoing, iterative process. In their study of strategic and competitive analysis Craig Fleisher and Babette Benoussan[9] put forward a range of insights that are pertinent here. To begin with, they highlight how organisational leaders have problems defining the environment that is relevant to them and staking out its domain. They note that despite the rhetoric around globalisation, organisational decision-makers can still have narrow, limited or invalid preoccupations about the environment that matters to them. They might think in terms of their sector or national context yet fail to grasp the importance of more profound global developments.

The economic crisis of 2008 is a graphic example of why this wider view matters. Bad debt in the United States' sub-prime mortgage market led to the collapse of some of the world's largest financial institutions. This resulted in an economic crisis that is still having a profound impact on organisations across the globe. This seismic economic shock demonstrates how events that occur outside of an organisation's own country and beyond the boundaries of its sector can still have fundamental implications, whether it operates in the private, public or non-governmental organisation (NGO) sector. It also highlights the powerlessness of an organisation when faced with the dynamics of globalisation and modern capitalism.[10]

The forces that shaped the 2008 economic crisis can be categorised as part of what Fleisher and Benoussan call the general environment. These are broad in scope, have long-lasting implications for organisational strategy and are regarded as beyond the control of any single organisation. As highlighted in Chapter 10, this landscape can be segmented into more manageable sub-sets such as economic, political, information, social, technological, legal and environmental factors. These are the forces that come together to create the weather system that affects the organisation. Contextual intelligence in this realm is about analysis, interpretation and thinking through appropriate organisational responses. Just as a yachtsman cannot control the weather neither can organisational leaders. The focus becomes about collecting data and using this to shape decision-making. Are prevailing conditions in our favour? Do we need to change course? Should we batten down the hatches in order to ride out the storm?

Mayo and Nohria[11] argue that the best leaders have an ability to understand these forces and how they shape the context they operate in, as well as an ability to seize the opportunities they present. They found that contextual intelligence at this big-picture level proved to be universally pivotal to the success of one thousand prominent United States business leaders in the twentieth century. Although their sample was dominated by Fortune 100 executives, they also set out to capture insights from the not-for-profit sector, as well as the leaders of successful small businesses. They contend that while many contextual factors are at play within a given era, six factors are particularly important in shaping the contextual landscape within the organisation's general environment: government intervention, global events, demographics, technology, labour and social mores.

Another insight generated by their research is the importance of synthesis. The successful leaders they studied were adept at bringing together a disparate raft of information to create an interpretation of the zeitgeist that was relevant for their organisation. Literally translated from German, zeitgeist means the spirit of the age and its society. It refers to the world view of an identified group of people at a particular moment in time and seeks to capture the general cultural, intellectual and moral climate of an era.[12] This contextual understanding can be shaped into a narrative that can be used as a litmus test to guide strategic decision-making. A good example of this is the discourse of turbulence and austerity that is currently permeating business, government and the NGO sector in Europe and North America.

A case study

A limitation of Mayo and Nohria's analysis is that it focuses on the intuitive gifts and contextual sensitivities of individual business leaders. Beyond calling for the recruitment of leaders with an outlook that is compatible with the prevailing context, they do not discuss how businesses should be structured and organised to scan the environment, interpret its most important attributes and plan accordingly. Grunig and Hunt's[13] key contribution to our field was to argue that the boundary spanning, intelligence gathering role is best carried out by public relations. A case study follows that charts how one organisation has attempted to systemise this activity.

The European Aeronautic Defence and Space Company (EADS) is made up of businesses such as the aircraft manufacturer Airbus, Eurocopter and EADS Astrium, the European leader in space programmes. In the wake of the 2008 economic crisis the company initiated a review of the way it monitored the external environment. It commissioned Echo Research in the UK to develop a qualitative and quantitative tool that could scan the media landscape for early signs of issues that might affect its future operations and reputation. The methods used were shaped by a belief that such global media evaluation might have highlighted an increase in reporting of the sub-prime mortgage issue in the United States before it became a crisis. EADS therefore asked Echo to include quantitative statistics on the themes and topics being explored in its existing qualitative issue forecast report. The objective was to track the changes in reporting volume as well as tone. The additional quantitative analysis was based on 52 global business and financial media.

The purpose of this additional sample was to act as a bellwether. For example, should the analysis detect an increase in reporting on trade agreements and import duties this may highlight a shift towards protectionism. Similarly, increased reporting on battery-powered trains or cars could indicate a reduced need for aircraft in the future. Echo conducted weekly searches in the 52 selected media for total mentions on topics such as the economy, environment, transport, globalisation, fuel and energy, corporate ethics, space, international relations and international markets. Each topic was then divided into sub-categories. In the case of international markets these were trade agreements, the World Trade Organization, import duties, export control and government subsidies.

This weekly quantitative data then informed the focus of a qualitative report. This analysis included an overview of the most prevalent topics and highlighted key reputational risks and opportunities. The data was discussed and challenged by an internal panel of EADS experts before being presented to the company's management team. A trend and issues analysis brief was then circulated to the company's top 50 executives. The findings of this report were combined with the results of opinion polling among the organisation's internal experts, as well as a network of external observers. The quantitative breakdown of media coverage by issues, informed by the results of the external polling, provided a sense of the relative strength of sentiment outside of the company towards a broad range of topics. Differences in emphasis, or perception gaps that might become issues for the company were identified and informed the communication strategy.

The EADS case study highlights how an organisation can respond to the issues generated by its general environment. Through a mixed bag of intelligence the company sought to better understand its context. The quantitative data provided the architecture around which strategic conversations could take place about the environmental issues facing the organisation. The fusing of this aspect of the research with the expert opinions and judgements of stakeholders helped to generate a rich picture that could aid organisational sense making. The focus for the organisation then becomes how to actively use these insights to initiate learning, innovation and adaptation. As Sternberg highlighted contextual intelligence predicates some form of action in response to environmental challenges: changing yourself, seeking to change the environment, or moving to another context.

Focusing on your value chain and generating actionable insight

The value chain is the part of the organisation's eco-system that contains more specific and immediate impacts for leaders (also see Chapter 5). The key players in this sphere are customers, service users, suppliers, groups and individuals who provide money or labour, competitors and partners. Understanding the issues that matter to these important stakeholder groups is vital. The value chain, unlike the general environment, offers the opportunity for organisations to influence and shape a more familiar landscape in pursuit of their own legitimate interests. The emphasis therefore shifts from the reactive organisational learning required of the general environment to active engagement.

The relationships forged in the value chain can also enhance an organisation's understanding of the world beyond these core stakeholders. Raymond Van Wijik and colleagues[14] found that high-performing organisations sit in a wide external network in order to be at the forefront of change. This allows them to identify, assimilate and apply new external knowledge within the organisation, as well as resulting in enhanced levels of innovation and financial performance. Furthermore, an understanding of the general environment and the role this plays in shaping the zeitgeist can guide organisational interactions in the value chain. In this environment the focus on engagement highlights the importance of organisations communicating in a way that is in tune with the times. Context is inherent in communication and to engage effectively organisations must ensure that their content addresses the preoccupations of stakeholders at the time of communication.[15] Content represents the point at which the sender and receiver of communication meet and meaning is generated by this interaction. To engage effectively, it is necessary to use the contextual intelligence that has been gathered to assess communication content before it is disseminated. The questions below, for example, can be used to decide whether or not an organisation has begun to develop a compelling piece of content:[16]

* *Salience*: Will what we have to say stand out with stakeholders?
* *Empathy*: Does the content relate to their hopes and fears?
* *Timeliness*: Is it what they want to consider at this precise moment?

- *Accessibility*: Is the content in the tone, style and place they want, or will respond to best?
- *Credibility*: Do we have the authority or appropriate knowledge to engage on the issue?
- *Feasibility*: Is what we are asking them to do possible and/or desirable?

To illustrate the above, it is worth considering how one of the UK's leading retailers responded to the challenge of contextual sensitivity. To enhance its capacity in this area ASDA[17] initiated a quarterly consumer survey. It focused on ten issues that impact on people's personal lives, including personal finance, relationships, education, safety from crime, job security, the environment, time pressure, diet, exercise and the economy. The research attempts to go beyond the consumption data usually generated by retailers and seeks to generate a more rounded view of consumer attitudes. Drawing on insight from the survey, ASDA announced in 2008 that its fashion brand would no longer be using celebrities to endorse its clothing products. The company noted that this change of strategy had been informed by its consumer research. The survey had highlighted a shift in sentiment away from celebrity culture during a time of economic hardship. Instead of featuring celebrities, the company's next fashion campaign featured three health workers from a collection of London hospitals.

ASDA provides an example of how an organisation can generate insight and act upon it. This is what Steyn[18] refers to as the qualitative aspects of the organisation; that is, taking into account the opinions, judgements and feelings of stakeholders within the context of the environment in which the organisation operates. This sensitivity is, in turn, influenced by an understanding of the general environment and the role this plays in shaping the overall mood or zeitgeist. In short, public relations leaders are required to play a zeitgeist leadership role, centralising and synthesising information for a wide spectrum of decision-making.

Summary

To meet the leadership challenges generated by the external environment this chapter has emphasised the importance of a strategic mindset that embraces uncertainty; effective process in terms of gathering information; the need for a web of intelligence; and contextually sensitive communication content. These components come together to support a process that Steyn frames as problem solving in unstructured situations.[19] They also reinforce the importance of stakeholders as a significant organisational asset and underline the strategic role of public relations within organisations. Nevertheless, the ambiguity inherent in this insight should also strike an important note of caution. It highlights how public relations practitioners will only have an incomplete and imperfect knowledge about what might occur in their organisational environment. This underlines the need for public relations leaders to learn, change and quickly adapt in the face of random and unknowable outcomes.

Notes

1 Sternberg, R.J. (1985). *Beyond IQ: A Triarchic Theory of Intelligence.* Cambridge: Cambridge University Press.
2 Moss, D. and Warnaby, G. (2003). Strategy and public relations. In Moss, D. Verčič, D. and Warnaby, G. (eds), *Perspectives on Public Relations Research* (pp. 59–85). London: Routledge.
3 Mintzberg, H. (2000). *The Rise and Fall of Strategic Planning.* London: Pearson Education.
4 For an entertaining and enlightening discussion of fuzzy issues, see Grint, K. (1997). *Fuzzy Management: Contemporary Ideas and Practices at Work.* Oxford: Oxford University Press.
5 Hubbard, D. (2007). *How to Measure Anything: Finding the Value of Intangibles in Business.* Hoboken, NJ: John Wiley.
6 For a comprehensive overview of how this and other ideas from complexity science are influencing management research see Allen, P., Macguire, S. and McKelvey, B. (eds) (2011). *The SAGE Handbook of Complexity and Management.* London: SAGE.
7 See Gilpin, D.R. and Murphy, P.J. (2008). *Crisis Management in a Complex World.* Oxford: Oxford University Press, as well as Gilpin, D.R. and Murphy, P.J. (2010). Implications of complexity theory for public relations: beyond crisis. In Heath, R. L. (ed.), *The SAGE Handbook of Public Relations* (pp. 71–83). Thousand Oaks, CA: Sage.
8 Weick is the leading authority on the subject of sensemaking. For a good introduction to his work see Weick, K.E. (2001). *Making Sense of the Organisation.* Oxford: Blackwell.
9 Fleisher, C.S. and Bensoussan, B. (2002). *Strategic and Competitive Analysis: Methods and Techniques for Analyzing Business Competition.* Harlow: Prentice Hall.
10 Far from being a left-wing critique this was one of the key preoccupations of the business and political leaders who gathered at the World Economic Forum in Davos, 25–29 January 2012.
11 Mayo, A.J. and Nohria, N. (2005). Zeitgeist leadership, *Harvard Business Review,* 83(10), 45–60.
12 Hegel developed the concept of the zeitgeist in the nineteenth century following the work of German Romantic philosophers such as Johann Gottfried and Cornelius Jagdmann.
13 Grunig, J.E. and Hunt, T.T. (1984). *Managing Public Relations.* Austin, TX: Holt, Rinehart & Winston.
14 Van Wijk, R., Jansen, J. and Lyles, M. (2008). Inter and intra-organisational knowledge transfer: a meta-analytic review and assessment of its antecedents and consequences, *Journal of Management Studies,* 45(4), 830–53.
15 MacManus, T. (2003). Public relations: the cultural dimension. In Moss, D., Verčič, D. and Warnaby, G. (eds), *Perspectives on Public Relations Research* (pp. 159–78). London: Routledge.
16 This interrogation process adopts Gregory's thinking on the presentation of messages. See Gregory, A. (2010). *Planning and Managing Public Relations Campaigns: A Strategic Approach.* London: Kogan Page. Willis has specifically highlighted the importance of this litmus test in the context of community engagement. See Willis, P. (2012). Engaging communities: Ostrom's economic commons, social capital and public relations, *Public Relations Review,* 38(1), 116–22.
17 ASDA is the UK's third largest supermarket group and part of Wal-Mart, the world's largest retailer and the biggest company in terms of sales.
18 Steyn, B. (2003). From strategy to corporate communication strategy: a conceptualisation, *Journal of Communication Management,* 8(2), 168–83.
19 Steyn, B. (2003). From strategy to corporate communication strategy (see above).

7 Valuing values

Introduction

The centrality of organisational values was highlighted in the model of the strategic role of public relations given in Chapter 5. Values are the organisation's 'true north', its point of reference. Values should be the touchstone for all its decision-making at every level; society, corporate, value chain and in its business functions.

This chapter is the companion to the next one on ethics. The values of an organisation underpin its approach to ethics and ethical considerations influence the framing of some value statements. Values are almost a standard item for most organisations. Go to any corporate website, whether it be for private, public or not-or-profit organisations, and the corporate values are likely to be on display along with the mission and vision. It will also be observed that there appears to be a corporate lexicon of values with themes and words such as innovation, integrity, sustainability and customer-service appearing regularly. The topic of values is enormous and any online search will reveal thousands of papers, pages and people with important things to say. All this chapter can do is make an introduction and offer a point of view that will help those with public relations leadership positions think through and provide arguments for values being *the* guide to organisational integrity. This chapter will cover six key areas:

- Values and the organisation
- Defining values
- Why values are important
- Develop values
- Making values real
- Implications for public relations leaders

Values and the organisation

As has been said already in this book, the world is becoming increasingly complex and organisations have to make sense of and deal with that complexity. Public relations leaders are at the heart of making sense of complexity, and are looked to for advice on how to cope with the growing amount of accountability that organisations face from a host of empowered stakeholders. The mantras of efficiency and profitability as the drivers of organisational decision-making are being questioned[1, 2] especially in the wake of the recent economic crisis in the northern hemisphere. Indeed, the moral leadership of corporate organisations is being challenged, a situation worsened by what is seen as excesses in senior executive pay and the possibly criminal nature of activities by the investment arm of large banks including the manipulation of interbank rates which was uncovered in 2012.[3] The criticism being levelled at organisations who find themselves being condemned is that there is something deeply flawed in their culture and character: that there is a dissonance between their espoused values of integrity and customer service and their behaviour which appears to indicate counter values of personal greed and increased profits at all costs. Values indicate what the culture should be while corporate behaviours indicate what the culture actually is: a point that will be returned to later in this chapter.

Referring again to what was said in Chapter 2, organisations are constructed through communication. Individuals collaborate through communication to achieve a particular purpose. That purpose and accompanying sense of direction requires communication to be agreed in the first place, then ongoing discussion to obtain, and sustain the support and commitment of those on whom the organisation depends. In this sense an organisation can be defined as people in a network who communicate. Over time, organisations develop a 'character' which is identifiable and unique to them. As the Arthur W. Page Society report *Building Belief* says, 'character refers to the enterprise's unique identity, its differentiating purpose, mission and values'.[4] Corporate character arises from an organisation's history and evolves over time, but according to Page, 'it must include the enterprise's enduring purpose – what it exists uniquely to do in the world – as well as the values and principles that guide the daily decisions and behaviour of everyone associated with it'.[5] It is of course the acting out of those decisions and behaviours that is the difficult part and the true test of organisational character.

Victoria von Groddeck's insight is that 'organisations perpetuate themselves by connecting decisions to decisions' and indeed can be described as 'decision machines'.[6] Guiding those decisions, ensuring consistency and perpetuating organisational character are values, either explicit or implicit. Shared values provide a platform around which staff in an organisation can coalesce, forming a sense of community and belonging and the yardstick for behaviour which is a great leveller. When genuinely shared they apply equally to everyone, giving a sense of common identity, common standards and common responsibility. These commonalities are how an organisation comes to be recognised in the world; values are the heart of corporate identity and they form the basis for coherent brands.[7] They are the 'beating heart' of the organisation according to Cees van Riel and Charles Fombrum,[8] and as Nicolas Ind, an acknowledged identity guru, says, 'a corporate brand is more than just the outward manifestation of an organisation – its name, logo, visual presentation. Rather it is the core of values that define it'.[9] It is small wonder then that values have become ubiquitous in organisations over recent years. They provide a constant in the dynamic world and a point of stability even though the organisation itself can go through major change.

Defining values

Having set the context with a discussion about organisations and values generally, it is now appropriate to focus on values themselves.

There is relatively common agreement on what values are.[10] They are beliefs, principles or concepts which lead to outcomes that the organisation sees as desirable. They set standards and behaviours that guide the way things should be done and frame how decisions should be made.

There are various categories of values, the best known probably being that of Milton Rokeach,[11] who at the personal level identified 18 terminal values (which are what you want to get out of life) and 18 instrumental values (which are ways to achieve terminal values). Examples of terminal values include a comfortable life, freedom, health, self-respect and instrumental values include ambitious, independent, capable and self-controlled. Similar categories of values could well be used by organisations. Terminal values could be *financially stable*, an *employer of choice* and *held in high esteem,* with instrumental values being *customer satisfaction, empowering employees* and *champion of the community.* Kenneth Kernaghan devised four categories of values for public services: ethical, democratic, professional and people.[12] An interesting categorisation for the private sector comes from Richard Barrett,[13] who says that values can be grouped under six headings. The first three are based on organisational needs: corporate survival (financial or growth indicators); corporate fitness (systems and processes); and customer/supplier relations (market share, brand loyalty, customer satisfaction and collaboration). The second three include the so-called 'soft stuff' that supports these front-line needs: corporate evolution (product and service innovation); corporate culture (vision, mission and values and employee fulfilment); and society/community contribution (social and environmental responsibility). While there might be an argument about the ordering of these values and about whether the 'soft stuff' is as soft as is implied, this categorisation demonstrates perfectly that not all values need be ethical in character. They are the actual beliefs/concepts that influence choices and decisions and it is perfectly acceptable to have financial and other kinds of values. As discussed in the next chapter, values are determined by the organisation, so there are no constraints, apart from the law or public opinion, about what these values should be. It goes almost without saying that it is pointless having values which cannot then be enacted.

There are some important differences between values and other properties or tools that an organisation promotes.

First, values are very personal: they belong to people. They commit those who espouse them and any failure in consistency to act by them compromises individuals personally.

Second, although they may be propounded by an organisation, they are not *owned* by it. They come alive when shared with others such as employees, the local community and customers. They are usually quite ambiguous and open to interpretation; indeed, this is one of their strengths, as they are inclusive because of their very ambiguity.

Third, they are enduring. They have a history and they give a promise for the future. True, organisations can revise and evolve their values; indeed, they should as the organisation changes and develops, but they form the basis of the corporate narrative and are for the long term. Any changes should be seen to be a natural progression, unless the organisation takes a deliberate and drastic turn away from them, which is full of risk. A product can be replaced, premises vacated, people come and go, but values are part of the organisational DNA which remains constant.

There is also a large difference between values-based organisations and rules-based or compliance-based organisations. Values do not say *how* something should be done or decided, but they provide, as Victoria von Groddeck says,[14] points for reflection which enhances innovation and responsibility rather than checklist compliance. Indeed, there is a very good argument that too much compliance-thinking removes personal responsibility as ticking the box *becomes* the responsibility. Furthermore, heavy compliance monitoring can have unfortunate unintended consequences. The Arthur W. Page Society report *The Dynamics of Public Trust in Business*[15] notes the findings of a major airline which discovered that their compliance monitoring of high levels of customer service was leading flight attendants to distrust and fear the very passengers that they were caring for, suspecting that some passengers may be managers masquerading as customers to check their performance. In distinction to this, there is evidence[16] that values-based organisations can move beyond compliance to a point where relationships, trust and mutual good come to the fore to the greater satisfaction of employees and to the benefit of the organisation. Organisations with a solid values base, lived out in practice, are forgiven much and supported when under threat. When the much loved UK retailer Marks & Spencer was under threat in the early 2000, customers and staff rallied around to support it, largely because of what it stood for, how it treated its own people and the trust built up over generations.

Why values are important

Having discussed values and organisations and defined values and their unique nature it is timely to look at why values are important. The four levels of accountability given in the model in Chapter 5 provide an excellent starting point:

Societal: the context in which organisations are operating is changing rapidly. The organisation behind the brand is becoming as important if not more important than the products which bear the brand name. Values are a way of linking organisations to wider society. They are a powerful point of connection. They are a way of brokering a rapprochement between the pursuit of organisational objectives and wider social concerns. They form a 'contract' between an organisation and society. For example, the six values which are embodied in the UK National Health Service (NHS) Constitution, a document enshrined in legislation, form the basis of the contract with the general public of the UK and 'provide common ground for cooperation to achieve shared aspirations'. These values are given in Figure 7.1. Organisational values that are congruent with society's values build legitimacy which in turn creates a store of goodwill in the community – social capital.

NHS values

Patients, public and staff have helped develop this expression of values that inspire passion in the NHS and should guide it in the 21st century. Individual organisations will develop and refresh their own values, tailored to their local needs. The NHS values provide common ground for co-operation to achieve shared aspirations.

Respect and dignity. We value each person as an individual, respect their aspirations and commitments in life, and seek to understand their priorities, needs, abilities and limits. We take what others have to say seriously. We are honest about our point of view and what we can and cannot do.

Commitment to quality of care. We earn the trust placed in us by insisting on quality and striving to get the basics right every time: safety, confidentiality, professional and managerial integrity, accountability, dependable service and good communication. We welcome feedback, learn from our mistakes and build on our successes.

Compassion. We respond with humanity and kindness to each person's pain, distress, anxiety or need. We search for the things we can do, however small, to give comfort and relieve suffering. We find time for those we serve and work alongside. We do not wait to be asked, because we care.

Improving lives. We strive to improve health and well-being and people's experiences of the NHS. We value excellence and professionalism wherever we find it – in the everyday things that make people's lives better as much as in clinical practice, service improvements and innovation.

Working together for patients. We put patients first in everything we do, by reaching out to staff, patients, carers, families, communities, and professionals outside the NHS. We put the needs of patients and communities before organisational boundaries.

Everyone counts. We use our resources for the benefit of the whole community, and make sure nobody is excluded or left behind. We accept that some people need more help, that difficult decisions have to be taken – and that when we waste resources we waste others' opportunities. We recognise that we all have a part to play in making ourselves and our communities healthier.

Figure 7.1 The NHS constitution statement of values

Source: NHS Constitution for England (2012 edition): www.dh.gov.uk/prod_consum_dh/groups/dh_digitalassets/@dh/@en/documents/digitalasset/dh_132958.pdf

Corporate: at corporate level values provide a guide to decision-making. This ensures that decisions are not taken purely for financial or other reasons, but are checked against the range of values to ensure that the organisation is acting 'in character'. Financial viability is of course a common and sensible value and organisations have to take tough financial decisions, but those decisions and consequent actions have to be taken within the context of other organisational values if legitimacy is to be maintained. For example, if another organisational value is *treating employees with respect,* then informing them of an organisational restructure via e-mail in management-speak is a betrayal of the most fundamental contract with staff. Taking decisions at this corporate level according to organisational values also means they can be explained more readily as the demand for organisational transparency increases, both internally and externally.

Value chain: this is the level at which those close stakeholders interact with the organisation on a regular basis. Shared values form the basis for trustful interactions. As discussed in the next chapter, as originally conceived, stakeholding is a deeply moral concept where 'the ends of cooperative activity and the means of achieving those ends'[17] become the subject of critical scrutiny. An issue arises where one party is more powerful than some of its stakeholders. This is where the practical benefit of shared values becomes apparent. Values embrace mutuality where risks and opportunities are borne by both parties[18] and where the vulnerability of the weaker party is limited.

Functional: values start at home. For public relations leaders there is an opportunity to demonstrate organisational values in their functional areas of responsibility. In research conducted by one of us[19] it was clear that board-level practitioners have a very clear set of values both personally and in their departments and that they see this as giving them the permission to challenge organisational behaviour and decisions that go against those agreed norms.

There are other benefits from identifying values that are meaningful:

As indicated earlier in this chapter, values are open to interpretation. This elasticity means that the complexity of the modern world and the different interpretations that people may have of values can be accommodated. The very ambiguity of values ironically brings an umbrella of meaning which has the ability to be transformative. As people reflect on values they find themselves in a learning cycle that provides space for actions and decisions that go beyond compliance. A self-reflective organisation is a learning organisation; it is an innovatory and self-refreshing organisation.

Values as lived by one organisation with its own character are very difficult to imitate. We know this because mergers often flounder as it is very difficult to bring together two cultures, even in similar industries. They are, therefore, a point of differentiation and can be levered to gain competitive advantage. Organisations such as Innocent drinks, IKEA and Virgin have built brands based on a very distinctive set of values which are lived out in action.

Internally values create a sense of shared identity and community. The role of leadership is critically important here. Employees have a sharp sense of what integrity in management looks like and seek for some sort of congruence with their own sense of morality. They also have a strong view of what is fair. Management legitimacy is reinforced when leaders are seen to have integrity and are fair in the way procedures and policies are enforced. This applies not only at the individual level, but to groups.

This discussion leads to an obvious next question: how can meaningful values be developed?

Developing values

When developing a set of values honesty is required to answer two questions: first, what is the *purpose* of the values and, second, are they *actual* values or ones that can be *aspired* to? Having clarity on those two issues requires intense and difficult discussions at all levels in the organisation; understanding the starting point is vital.

On the first point, as Gary Weaver and Linda Trevino say about strong values and ethics,[20] they can be used as a control system – creating order and management control by enforcing behavioural compliance. Alternatively, values can align with employees' own values and needs and therefore elicit support because staff identify with them. Of course these stances are not mutually exclusive. Values by definition are meant to be a control and prompt for behaviour and if people within the organisation do not comply with them they (values or people) should be challenged. Complementary to this, if those values also align with employees' (and other stakeholders') values then they are likely to be willingly supported. An interesting observation that we have made is that when employees are recruited they are rarely asked if they can actively support organisational values. Maybe an honest discussion at this stage would help both sides make an informed decision.

The second point is more complex. Of course it is meaningless, indeed dangerous, to have values that do not reflect reality, but for most organisations values are also aspirational. They are indicators of how the organisation *aspires* to behave as well as how it should behave now. In management it is always tempting to have values that are counsels of perfection. The truth is that values will not always be lived up to because organisations are made up of people who are not perfect. Indeed, the idea of 'flawsome' brands,[21] those that have flaws, but are still awesome, just like human beings, is gaining traction. Brands and organisations with personality are attractive and if they have the humility to admit where they get things wrong, the public can be forgiving.

There are two other key factors that need to be considered when developing values:

It takes time. The organisation has to go through a period of reflection and self-examination. As mentioned earlier, values are the core of the organisation, its DNA. Deep reflection is constitutive, that is, it determines what the organisation *is* and *will be*, and that in turn will determine what it *does* – its actions and behaviours. Extended discussion and a consensus around what the values can and should be and what they mean, remembering that elasticity is required, is needed to capitalise on the richness of interpretation which gives liberty to individuals to express and live them in a way that is real to them.

These discussions should involve not only people inside the organisation, but be tested with external stakeholders to see if actual or potential values ring true. One of us has written in detail on how this may be done,[22] but in essence this involves a delicate negotiation where proposed values, surfaced internally through a process of deliberation, are exposed to external stakeholders who in turn provide feedback requiring action which may involve adjustment of values, or even strategy or mission. In this sense the whole organisation goes through a constant process of learning and the corporate identity or brand evolves and develops over time. This allows for values to develop too and the story of the organisation progresses and advances as it changes through constant interaction with its stakeholders. Dialogue is at the heart of this. However, in the age of social media, leadership requires not just dialogue (communication between the organisation and other parties) but, in the words of Nada and Andrew Kakabadse, polylogue consists of 'ceaseless conversations, negotiations, compromise, mutual exploration and enquiry where the range of participants encompassed not only covers the trusted but also the "strange and alien voices" '.[23] To this can be added that these conversations take place concurrently and between all parties.

Leading these discussions is a role for the most senior management, preferably the CEO, but the public relations leader has a crucial part to play in facilitating them, seeing through the necessary actions and of course leading some discussions personally if they are in the senior management team.

In practical terms there are a number of useful tools[24] that can be used to identify actual values and to test existing ones. Just two which we have used extensively are explained here.

The first is the cobweb technique. A cobweb showing the NHS values is given in Figure 7.2 and has been used by us with a number of NHS organisations to test whether values are lived. The technique is best used with different groups and individuals both within and outside the organisation to rank how they perceive the organisation's performance. The results open up opportunities for discussion about similarities and differences in perception between groups and the degree of difference. But more than this, it invites deep reflection on organisational behaviour internally and externally and on what needs to be reinforced or changed.

The cobweb can also be used to test proposed values in several ways by posing a series of questions such as: Do these values reflect the organisation now? Are these values ones that employees can ascribe to, make decisions by and act within now? Are they ones that can be aspired to? And, beyond that, what needs to be done to make them real? One of us has used this technique within a university to test an extended list of proposed values with those scoring least being removed.

The second technique discovers the real and lived values of organisations and is called *laddering*. This requires detailed interviewing of a selection of people, usually about 20, concerning up to five everyday actions or decisions they have undertaken at work in the last week. The interviewee is questioned on why they undertook their work in a particular way and why it was important. This continues, tracking back until the interviewer can find no other answers. A chain of means and ends is revealed with the motivations or values being uncovered at the end of the chain. This is not a simple procedure, but the aggregated results from those interviews are very telling. The condensed example given by Johan van Rekom and his colleagues[25] in Figure 7.3 shows the idea. The top levels of the map reveal the real values and motives at work.

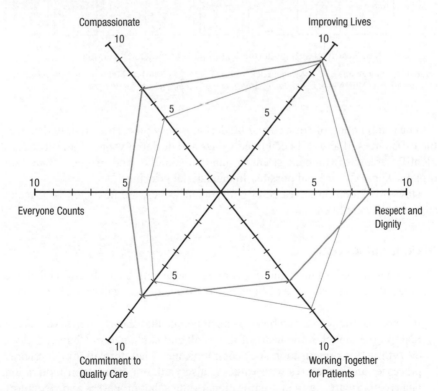

Figure 7.2 An example of an NHS spidergram completed by two different groups

Note: O = low score, 10 = high score

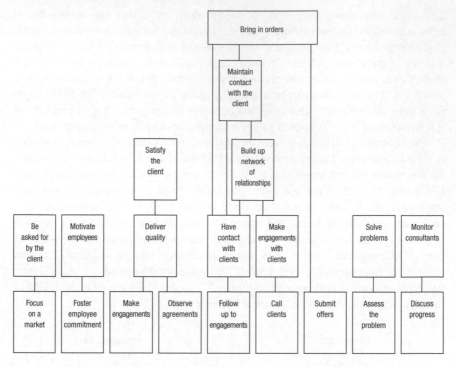

Figure 7.3 Van Rekom et al.'s laddering technique – a condensed version

Source: J. van Rekom, J., C.B.M. van Riel, and B. Wierenga (2006). A Methodology for Assessing Organisational Court Values. *Journal of Management Studies*, 43(2), 75–201

The combination of cobweb and laddering is very powerful: first, to discover the differences, if any, between lived values and declared values; but, second, to identify areas of hidden strength (and weakness) and deeper issues in organisational culture and possibly in managerial priorities.

Having decided on or tested organisational values, the next step is to make sure that they are lived.

Making values real

There are a number of tests and imperatives apart from the areas outlined above that the public relations leader can champion to ensure that values are kept real:

It is not just the words and behaviours of people that show whether values are real. As the model at the heart of this book and explained in Chapter 5 says, everything the organisation does communicates. Therefore aligning systems, processes and structures with values is also vital. For example, if motivation and creativity are claimed organisational values, but processes and structures are bureaucratic and managers constantly question creative ideas, these values will be stifled. The public relations leader is perfectly placed to identify and do something about these discrepancies. As one director of communications we know notes, 'My job is to fix the reality'.

Values audits usually take place at irregular intervals and are often prompted by a major event such as the arrival of a new CEO, a merger or significant change in direction. Values should be audited every year, both internally and externally, to determine whether they are still the touchstone of decision-making, relevant and lived. As indicated earlier, values do evolve over time, just as the values of individuals do, but they have deep provenance and are normally of considerable duration. The annual health check reveals progress in being a values-based organisation.

Values in action means that they restrain options as well as opening them up. Just because an organisation *can* do something doesn't mean it *should*. Values can be tested by an analysis of those things the organisation decides *not* to do as well as by what it does.

Values-based organisations have a character, an aura about them. The Arthur W. Page Society report *Building Belief*[26] encapsulates this in their model for corporate character. The test is: does it look like, sound like, think like, perform like an organisation that has values at the centre? If the answer to all these questions is *yes*, then the organisation will have the ring of authenticity about it. If the answer is *no*, the reality needs fixing.

We would argue that values-based organisations place a particular responsibility and centrality to the work and role of the public relations leader. This is indicated strongly in the model in Chapter 5 where the leader as orienter, navigator, catalyst and implementer are explained in detail. However, it is worth listing some additional implications for the public relations leader here.

Implications for public relations leaders

In recent years, much store has been laid on the importance of public relations leaders building the reputation or social capital of the organisation. Considerable emphasis has been placed on the ability of practitioners to 'fix' and manage *situations* which may build or threaten reputation, such as handling crises well or maintaining positive relationships with critical stakeholders. However, it is obvious from this chapter that managing reputation or perceptions of reputation is not enough. Values-based organisations require leaders who take responsibility for what the Arthur W. Page Society calls the 'organisational essence';[27] indeed, the public relations leader is the steward and curator of this. Their role is critical in building organisational character from the inside.

The director of communications who believed his role was to fix the reality meant that it was his job to identify all those points in the organisation's network where the organisational promise was not being lived up to and then to take the necessary steps to fix this.

First, then, public relations leaders are not just fixers of situations but fixers of organisations.

Second, public relations leaders are organisational *educators* (see also Chapter 13). They work with other leaders, managers and employees to help them understand the full extent of their public relations and relationship responsibilities, and educate them on the fact that everything they do and all the systems and processes they construct communicate their personal and the organisation's values. Beyond that, and as the first point implies, public relations leaders need to work with others to ensure that their decisions are within the values-base and character of the organisation.

Third, values displayed in behaviour and action can be effectively and powerfully enshrined in narratives – organisational stories. Values-based narratives have been used by organisations like IKEA[28] to position the company, explain its actions and generate support. These stories necessarily require the ring of truth about them, but they can also personalise and add warmth and character and bring values to life. Organisational history, whether that be in the private or public sector, provides a sense of place, continuity and stability when it forms the basis of the developing corporate narrative. A narrative that demonstrates steady and enduring values, even if they do evolve, provides a framework for an authentic voice. The whiskey manufacturer Jack Daniel's relates stories of the provenance of the company and of how its values have been maintained and provides a powerful example of this kind of narrative.

Fourth, mapping values and interests provides a clear indicator of where there are opportunities for fulfilling collaborations and where different types of relationship may be appropriate. Figure 7.4 illustrates this.

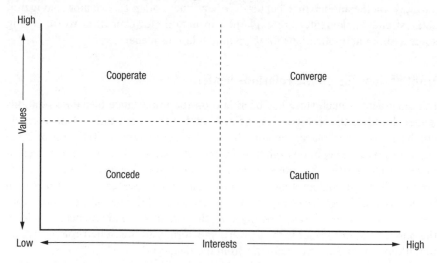

Figure 7.4 The values/interest matrix of collaboration

Where values and interests coincide there is convergence: mutual interests aligned with the value base offer opportunities for full collaboration.

If there is high coincidence of values, but interests are not shared, there are opportunities for cooperation. It may be, for example, the two organisations are operating in different markets or have different products, but shared values give them the basis for cross-support. Typical of this is where a charity links with an organisation.

Where interests are high, but values are not aligned, caution is required. The organisation opens itself up to possible 'contamination' from an association with others whose values may be very different. An example of this may be an association with a business partner who has access to a new and lucrative market, but whose business methods are suspect. Links with activist groups can also fall into this category. By definition their interests in an issue may be common, but the difference in values puts them in a position of natural opposition to the organisation. While understanding the dangers inherent in this position there can be fruitful collaborations. For example npower partnered with Greenpeace to promote green energy. In many ways the dangers are greater for the activist group who may find their ability to voice their opposition becomes compromised, or that they are seen to have been 'turned' by corporate organisations who are using them.

It is a test of true character when an organisation of any kind resists a large opportunity because it does not 'fit' with its values.

Where neither values nor interests are shared, then it is best for both parties to concede that working together is not going to be fruitful, although being open to dialogue is important given that situations and organisations change.

Summary

This chapter has provided a rationale for organisations to examine their values in a new light and to see this as an opportunity to create shared value. In an increasingly complex and diverse world values can provide an anchor point around which stakeholders can coalesce. They can provide meaning and direction for employees and leaders as they make decisions and they can provide both organisational differentiation and personal identification for external stakeholders. They are the basis for organisational character and the living of them in practice provides the basis of authenticity. As Yves Daccord, CEO of the International Committee of the Red Cross, says: 'The days of Corporate Social Responsibility are past, we need to move to CSV ... Creating Shared Values.'[29]

Notes

1 Tencati, A. and Zsolnai, L. (2009). The collaborative enterprise, *Journal of Business Ethics*, 85(3), 367–76.
2 Pruzan, P. (1998). From control to values based management and accountability, *Journal of Business Ethics*, 17, 1379–94.

3 For information on the Libor scandal see www.bbc.co.uk/news/business-18671255.
4 Arthur W. Page Society (2012). *Building Belief: A New Model for Activating Corporate Character and Authentic Advocacy* (p. 5). Available at awpagesociety.com
5 Arthur W. Page Society (2012). *Building Belief* (see above).
6 Von Groddeck, V. (2011). Rethinking the role of value communication in business corporations from a sociological perspective – why organisations need value-based semantics to cope with societal and organisational fuzziness, *Journal of Business Ethics*, 100, 69–84.
7 Tarnovskaya, V.V. and de Chernatony, L. de (2011). Internalising a brand across cultures: the case of IKEA, *International Journal of Retail & Distribution Management*, 39(8), 598–618.
8 One of the standard texts on corporate communication from a management perspective is Van Riel, C.B.M. and Fombrum, C.J (2007). *Essentials of Corporate Communication*. Abingdon: Routledge.
9 Nicolas Ind, quoted in Edvardsson, B., Enquist, B. and Hay, M (2006). Values-based service brands: narratives from IKEA, *Managing Service Quality*, 16(3), 230–46.
10 A good explanation of values can be found in Shaw, P. (2006). *The Four Vs of Leadership: Vision, Values, Value-added, Vitality*. Chichester: Capstone Publishing Ltd. In Collins, J.C. and Porras, J.I (2004). *Built to Last: Successful Habits of Visionary Companies*. London: Random House values are called the 'central and enduring tenets of the organisation' and the 'glue that holds an organisation together as it grows, decentralises, diversifies and expands'.
11 The full list of Rokeach's Terminal and Instrumental Values can be found at http://en.wikipedia.org/wiki/Rokeach_Value_Survey.
12 Kernaghan, K. (2003). In integrating values into public service: the values statement as centerpiece, *Public Administration Review*, 63(6), 711–18.
13 Barratt, R. (2006) *Building a Values-Driven Organization: A Whole System Approach to Cultural Transformation*. Oxford: Butterworth-Heinemann.
14 Von Groddeck, V. (2011). Rethinking the role of value communication in business corporations from a sociological perspective (see above).
15 Arthur W. Page Society (2012). *The Dynamics of Public Trust in Business-Emerging Opportunities for Leaders*. Available at awpagesociety.com.
16 Arthur W. Page Society (2012). *The Dynamics of Public Trust in Business-Emerging Opportunities for Leaders* (see above).
17 Arthur W. Page Society (2012). *The Dynamics of Public Trust in Business-Emerging Opportunities for Leaders* (see above).
18 For a discussion on the role of mutuality, balance of power and trust safeguards, see above (note 15).
19 Gregory, A. (2008). The competencies of senior practitioners in the UK: an initial study, *Public Relations Review*, 34(3), 215–23.
20 Weaver, G. and Trevino, L.K (1999). Compliance and values oriented ethics programs: influences on employees' attitudes and behavior, *Business Ethics Quarterly*, 9(2), 315 –35.
21 For an introduction on Flawsome Brands see www.trendwatching.com/trends/flawsome.
22 Gregory, A. (2007). Involving stakeholders in developing corporate brands: the communication dimension, *Journal of Marketing Management*, 23(1–2), 59–73.
23 Kakabadse, N. and Kakabadse, K. (2005). Discretionary leadership: from control/coordination to value co-creation. In Cooper, C.L. (ed.), *Leadership and Management in the 21st Century* (pp. 57–106). Oxford: Oxford University press, p. 91.
24 A good summary of these techniques is given in de Chernatony, L., Drury, S. and Segal-Horn, S. (2004). Illustrating sustaining services brands' values. *Journal of Marketing Communications,* 10, 73–93.

25 Van Rekom, J., van Riel, C.B.M. and Wierenga, B. (2006). A methodology for assessing organisational core values, *Journal of Management Studies*, 43(2), 75–201.
26 Arthur W. Page Society (2012). *Building Belief* (see above).
27 Arthur W. Page Society (2012). *Building Belief* (see above).
28 Edvardsson, B., Enquist, B. and Hay, M (2006). Values-based service brands: narratives from IKEA. *Managing Service Quality*, 16(3), 230–46.
29 Keynote speech, The CEO's view: the role of corporate communication in adding value to the organisation by Yves Daccord, Director General, ICRC International Committee of the Red Cross, Switzerland. Lac Leman Communication Forum, Communication and Leadership. Lausanne, Switzerland, September 2011.

8   The business of ethics

Introduction

In its 2012 Global Trust Barometer[1] Edelman found that trust in all four institutions it surveyed (government, business, NGOs and media) had fallen between 2011 and 2012. In fact, the number of sceptics had almost doubled, with the credibility of chief executive officers (CEOs) seeing the biggest decline of all in business. The same survey showed a 29 per cent negative gap between the importance business places on ethical business practices and how survey respondents believed they were performing. In recommending a way forward, the survey proposes that business needed to move to a position where they earned a licence to lead. At the top of the list for gaining that is through exercising principles-based leadership, not rules-based performance. In other words, values and ethical leadership is at the heart of gaining trust.

This chapter is the twin of the previous one on values. Organisational values should guide organisational action and this chapter will argue the case for consistency in approach with ethics being a major consideration when selecting values for the organisation. This mirrors personal life where ethics, the formalisation of codes of acceptable behaviour, are based partly on personal values and partly on other criteria such as societal norms and the law. On the face of it, this appears relatively straightforward – act according to organisational ethics and values and those actions should be regarded as ethical within the context of that organisation. Unfortunately, business life is not always as simple as that.

Business ethics concern behaviour and the judgements that are made about whether an action is good or bad, right or wrong. Ethical behaviour is about making choices. It is relatively easy to choose when an action is straightforwardly right or wrong, for example accepting a bribe or not (even this is not straightforward in some cultures), but it is far more difficult to choose where two apparent 'rights' or values conflict. For example, is it right, and not just contractual, to reward a highly successful CEO (however success is defined) when employees are being made redundant? What arguments does the communication leader make to justify the decision either way?

This chapter will explore the topic of ethics in four parts:

- Defining ethics and why values-based ethics are important
- Three ethical frameworks and an argument for values-based ethics
- Ethics and leadership
- Ethics and the organisation

Defining ethics

The words *morals* and *ethics* are often used interchangeably, but they are different. Morals are concerned with the *individual* and can be described as the principles or values by which a person lives their lives. These values will be arrived at not only through personal reflection, but by other influences such as parents, society, educational background and peers. Ethics concerns the 'study and codification of moral principles into *systematic frameworks* so that decisions can be made about what is right and wrong in a reasoned and structured way'.[2]

The two of course are linked and are particularly important for communication leaders who may be called on from time to time to defend an organisational action that conflicts with their own moral code. Trevino and Nelson make a clear link between morals and business ethics stating that ethical decision-making in organisations comprises three steps: moral awareness – recognising an ethical dilemma exists; moral judgement – deciding what is right; and ethical behaviour – doing the right thing.[3] It is of course *people* who make these decisions and, given that public relations professionals work at the point where issues collide,[4] it is often they who are caught in the middle of these dilemmas because they profoundly impact of relationships.

To protect and guide employees, organisations often have ethical codes which included areas where ethical conflicts may arise and sometimes provide guidance on how they should be handled. A famous example of this is the Johnson & Johnson Credo:

> We believe our first responsibility is to the doctors, nurses and patients, to mothers and fathers and all others who use our products and services...
>
> We are responsible to our employees, the men and women who work with us throughout the world...
>
> We are responsible to the communities in which we live and work...
>
> Our final responsibility is to our stockholders...[5]

However, unless these codes mean something in the day-to-day working of the organisation they are worthless.[6]

Ethics, therefore, have to be embedded in the DNA of an organisation. Otherwise they can be accused of being something that is 'tacked on' to current practices; something that forces minor adjustments to make things appear ethical.[7] In other words, ethics becomes instrumental and pragmatic rather than essential to organisational being and functioning.

So, what is the ethical basis for organisational being and functioning? As argued in the previous chapter, values are the DNA of the organisation – its thinking heart.[8] Just as personal values are the guide for personal choices and actions, organisational values should reflect the ethics of the organisation and be the basis of choices and actions for a number of reasons:

- Organisations choose values for themselves without coercion and it is legitimate to hold them to account against those values.
- Values are the public declaration of standards and how organisations measure up to them is a barometer of their moral health.
- Modern society is pluralistic and diverse, so are most organisations. Values are 'common starting points'[9] around which organisational identity can be built. Individuals who do not believe in those values face a moral choice about whether or not they should join the organisation.
- Adhering to a values-base rather than a rules-base allows individuals to express their personality while being assured their behaviours are acceptable: they provide direction and protection when ethical choices are made.
- 'Authenticity'[10] is a current watchword for organisational reputation. To be authentic means being the same on the inside as on the outside[11] otherwise stakeholders will detect a 'legitimacy gap'.[12] Authenticity 'requires a strong sense of self',[13] which in turn depends on a careful selection and reflection on values and ways of doing things. Shannon Bowen states that authenticity comprises three elements, transparency, truthfulness and genuineness,[14] and all three are deeply value-laden with strong ethical overtones.

Having covered the basics about what ethics is and why values-based ethics are important, it is now appropriate to move on to outline the main ethical frameworks because it is from these rational bases that moral judgements and ethical decision-making springs.

Three ethical frameworks

The most fundamental question in ethics is: is it possible to know right from wrong? There are two main schools of thought on this. Those who believe that there are actual and objective moral truths and absolutes (cognitivists)[15] and those who believe that morality is subjective or related to specific cultures and contexts (non-cognitivists). They contend there are no absolutes, just beliefs, attitudes and opinions. So, while giving gifts is seen as bribery in one culture, it is seen as honouring in another.

The non-cognitive school in public relations[16] contend that the *way* in which communication and debate takes place determines whether it is ethical or not. The integrity of dialogue is maintained by equity in the process which results in the outcome having moral authority. The 'rules' of ethical dialogue[17] include equality in setting the agenda and initiating and continuing dialogue, freedom to test, probe, challenge and explain without manipulation and equality of power. In return, participants have a duty to ensure that they are understood, are factually accurate, engage in a manner appropriate to those with whom they are conducting the dialogue and are sincere. The outcome is almost immaterial as long as there is a desire to find the negotiated truth since it is only through dialogue that truths can be arrived at.

While this might be seen as an ideal to be aspired to, most practitioners' experience of reality is different. Very often their task is to persuade, they have limited time in which to undertake discussions and the fact is that power is not evenly distributed. Moreover, most people believe that there *are* principles of actual right and wrong and it is on the basis of this that the following three ethical frameworks have become most prevalent.

Consequentialism

Deriving from the Greek word telos (end) and logos (the study of), teleological or consequentialist theories focus on the results or consequences of behaviour. The most best-known consequentialist theory is utilitarianism,[18] which proposes that actions be judged on their effects. A right act is one which results in more benefit (or happiness) than harm and indeed should seek to minimise harm and maximise benefit.

There are three main problems with this approach. First, it is not always possible to predict the consequences of actions fully or accurately. Relocating offices may have all manner of hidden consequences. Second, how are conflicting benefits to be reconciled? For example, being a good corporate citizen means that shareholder benefits may not be maximised in all cases. Third, utilitarianism can lead to 'ends justify the means' actions. So, it is ethical to displace rural communities in developing countries so that factories and roads can be built because that secures the happiness of the greatest number.

Despite these dangers, it is clearly foolish and, indeed, unethical to disregard the consequences of actions.

Non-consequentialism

Deontology, deriving from the Greek word deontos, meaning duty, proposes that ethical actions are based on obligations, principles and rights. Human beings should be treated with dignity and respect because they have rights. Decision-making is based on principles or values that transcend situations. Thus, the United Nations Universal Declaration of Human Rights[19] upholds deontological principles by stating that individuals have certain inalienable rights wherever they are and whatever their status.

Clearly, rights can only be upheld if others believe it is their duty to bestow those rights. Deontologists focus on those duties. The modern father of deontology is Immanuel Kant,[20] who proposed the principle of the 'Categorical Imperative'. This states that the test of ethical action is whether it would translate into a universal law which any other person faced with the same situation could follow. The moral law consists of applying transcendent principles,[21] which together are often simplified into the golden rule which is enshrined in most religions – do unto others as you would have them do unto you.

As with utilitarianism, there are three main problems with deontology. First, what happens if two universal principles clash? So, what is decided when the press have a legitimate interest in an employee, but a duty of care is owed to that employee? Second, what if keeping a universal law leads to bad consequences? So, keeping promises to employees about no redundancies means that the company loses competitive advantage. Third, what if there is no agreement about what the moral law is? Saving face is a deeply entrenched cultural norm in Asia. Does that mean that telling the truth is put to one side?

Again, despite the problems with deontology, few people would argue that acting on sound principles and a sense of duty is a bad moral code as long as it is not taken to extremes.

Virtue ethics

While consequentialism and non-consequentialism put a consideration of *right actions* centre stage, virtue ethics focuses on what it means to be a good person. How should one live the *good* life? Maximising benefits or acting in accordance with universal principles can appear to be rather nebulous, but most people recognise a good person and can describe their character traits.

Virtue ethics[22] were first systematically propounded by Aristotle – a barbarian living in Greece. His central thesis is that an individual becomes virtuous by practising the virtues and through practice those virtues become an engrained part of character. Aristotle described the four major virtues – wisdom, justice, courage and self-control – from which he extrapolated a longer list. Judgements about right and wrong have to be made in light of the character of the person undertaking action. An action is right if it is something a virtuous person would characteristically do in those circumstances. A virtuous person is a grounded individual who is self-aware, purposive, stable and reliable because at their core is a set of virtues that provides a steady moral compass. Over time Aristotle's virtues have been added to in various ways. For example, the original four, plus faith, hope and charity, make up the seven virtues of the Roman Catholic Catechism.

Aristotle's idea of virtue was that it was a mean between two extremes. Thus an excess of courage is rashness and a lack is cowardice. He is also sensitive to the fact that the mean along the rashness/cowardly continuum may shift depending on circumstances. His virtue ethics embraces the concept of phronesis, or practical wisdom which a virtuous person applies in given situations.

The main problem with virtue ethics is that it does not provide a guide for action; it focuses on how the individual may become good and the benefits that arise from being good – they have a sense of well-being. Hence, virtue ethics does not conflict with consequentialism or non-consequentialism. Indeed, virtue ethicists would say that developing the virtues for their own sake will help in making moral decisions when the time arrives.

So what is the relevance of this discussion to working practitioners? There are a number of points to be made here:

- Taking ethical decisions on behalf of the organisation requires a practitioner to 'reflectively examine his own beliefs, values and ethical decision-making paradigms'.[23]
- For personal virtue substitute organisational values. By living and practising organisation values they become part of the character of the organisation and an intrinsic guide for decision-making that has life in application in the day-to-day.
- It is self-evident that practitioners and indeed all managers have obligations or duties that they should discharge: to the law, to stakeholders, to their organisations, their professional bodies. Unfortunately, sometimes these conflict.
- There are many times when the consequences of an action must take precedence in ethical decision-making. A clear example of this is the need to protect employees against the consequences of press interest which is unjustified.
- Understanding ethical frameworks helps practitioners make logical, consistent decisions with a confidence that their decision-making process can be laid open to scrutiny if required.

Ethics and leadership

While the foregoing makes a relatively strong link between ethics and leadership, it is important to drill down into this topic a little deeper.

It may be a truism, but leaders set, maintain or change the culture of an organisation[24] and are usually role models that are emulated by more junior staff. Organisational founders are particularly influential in this regard; note Steve Jobs of Apple and Richard Branson of Virgin. However, all leaders at all levels influence culture[25] as they try to articulate the organisational vision and direction with peer and junior colleagues, by the way they make decisions and by what they are seen to hold as important and to value.

As the Edelman Trust Barometer alluded to earlier shows, trust in business leaders is low and the way forward is to demonstrate principled leadership. A principled leader has to make their principles visible and gain a reputation for ethical leadership. A survey in 2003[26] found that this reputation rests upon two dimensions that work in tandem: moral person and moral manager. The leader as moral person demonstrates certain traits (one might call them virtues): honesty, integrity and trustworthiness. Even more important is the way they behave to others – treating them with respect, been open and listening, doing the right thing and making decisions that are explicitly based on values such as fairness and a broader concern for society. However, the leader as moral person shows others how the *leader* is likely to behave. The leader as moral manager makes clear the expectations they have about the behaviour *of those they lead*. Moral leaders do this by being role models of ethical conduct, being open and frequent in their communication of values and ethics, by holding individuals to account for their conduct and by rewarding ethical behaviour.

Recent research undertaken by one of us[27] with board-level communication directors found that they all have a clear and articulated set of personal values. Interestingly, though, the public sector emphasised the ethics and conduct of the whole organisation to perform for the public good, whereas for the private sector there was more focus on personal standards. A possible explanation for this is that private-sector communicators regard themselves as the exemplar of ethical standards for their organisation and wish to perform a role as the 'ethical guardian' for the whole organisation by enacting those standards personally and within their departments.

A key characteristic of these leaders is also their moral courage.[28] They are unafraid to confront the most senior directors including the CEO and the chair of the board with awkward truths. In these situations, prescriptive codes of ethics or practice, whether organisational or professional, are not comprehensive enough or they recommend decision-making processes which are too simplified to deal with the multi-layered, complex and conflicting situations with which senior communicators are faced. For them, values-based codes are more helpful. For example the Seven Principles of Public Life,[29] which apply to all those in public service, provide a benchmark for decision-making.

Having looked at individual leaders and ethics it is now appropriate to look at the broader subject of ethics within organisations.

Ethics in the organisation

The modern conception of stakeholding[30] organisations has deep ethical overtones. Indeed

> stakeholder theory is distinct because it addresses morals and values explicitly as a central feature of managing organisations. The ends of cooperative activity and the means of achieving these ends are critically examined in stakeholder theory in a way that they are not in many theories of strategic management.[31]

Central to the idea of stakeholding is that both organisations and stakeholders can be defined in terms of their moral stake. A terrorist may take a stake in an organisation and destroy its premises; however, that stake is illegitimate and the organisation has no obligation to that individual. However, for those legitimate stakeholders, it is not unreasonable for them to understand the basis on which their relationship with the organisation will be conducted. A way organisations make this clear is through statements of customer compacts or mission, values and goals statements which describe not only what the purpose and objectives of the organisation are, but 'how they will behave along the way'.[32] One of the most comprehensive examples of this is the UK National Health Service (NHS)

Constitution,[33] which is in effect a compact with the whole of UK society and includes a detailed statement on NHS values (see Chapter 5 for more on this).

A key challenge for strategic public relations leaders is how a value-based, ethical approach translates into value for the organisation. Certainly the more recent forms of company reporting such as the Global Reporting Initiative[34] and the new International Integrated Reporting initiative[35] demonstrate the move away from a purely monetary evaluation of performance. High levels of complexity and uncertainty are beginning to convince business leaders that 'the narrow language of efficiency, control and profit' is insufficient and that what is required are 'multi dimensional and qualitative measures that explicitly recognise the values the organisation shares with its stakeholders'.[36] Of course, it is perfectly possible that the move to a values-based relationship with stakeholders can be used purely instrumentally, with an organisation using a new language and undertaking cynically motivated corporate social responsibility (CSR) projects in an attempt to maintain their legitimacy. However, from just a pragmatic point of view, these kinds of moves are usually quickly discovered – values are put to the test whenever a crisis looms. Values-based management takes into account a full stakeholder perspective, attempting to balance a range of stakeholders all with their own values and reasons for engaging with the organisation. As discussed in Chapter 7, the very act of prioritising stakeholders brings into play judgements about how valued each group are.

So, given all this, how practically can ethical judgements and decisions be made? There are several models that can be used to help in making consistent and values-based decisions.[37] Probably the most famous is the Potter box[38] developed by Ralph Potter, a social ethics professor at Harvard University (see Figure 8.1).

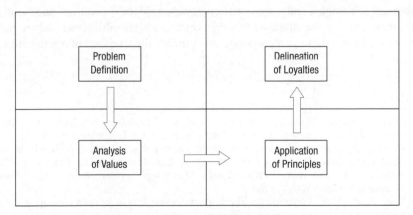

Figure 8.1 The Potter box

The Potter box is used as follows:

- *Problem*: the problem needs to be identified and defined accurately. Thus, gathering the facts about how the problem arose, what its elements are and the context are important, along with any emotional or other aspects that might be relevant.
- *Values*: what are the personal, organisational and professional values that are relevant? The values that are chosen will guide the nature of decision-making.
- *Principles*: what ethical frameworks will be employed to think through the problem; for example, will duties and responsibilities take precedence, or will the outcomes of the action have more weight, or will the motives and character of the person have some bearing?
- *Loyalties*: a decision on where the premier loyalty lies has to be taken. The loyalties will be to self, profession, organisation and/or society. The honourable tradition of whistleblowing is a difficult path to tread, but where society or stakeholders are put at risk by potential organisational decisions then there is a moral obligation on the public relations leader to take this route.

Summary

In terms of the model outlined in Chapter 5 and which is at the heart of this book, the four levels of societal, corporate, value chain and functional should be seen as levels of stakeholder obligation. It will be the test of the strategic public relations leader as to whether they discharge the duty to ensure that the stakeholder voice is heard, even if it is 'broader society'. That, and the careful balancing of complex and often conflicting stakeholder expectations and rightful demands, will be the mark of whether organisational ethics and values have value, or whether they are a corporate mask hiding the true face of organisational intent.

Notes

1 2012 Edelman Trust Barometer. London: Edelman. Available at http://edelmaneditions.com/wp-content/uploads/2012/01/Final-Brochure-1.16.pdf.
2 Gregory, A. (2009) Ethics and professionalism in public relations. In Tench, R. and Yeomans, E. (eds), *Exploring Public Relations*, 2nd edition. London: Pearson, p. 276.
3 Trevino, L.K. and K.A. Nelson (2004). *Managing Business Ethics*, 3rd edition. Hoboken, NJ: John Wiley & Sons.
4 Pearson, R. (2000) Beyond ethical relativism in public relations. In Grunig, J.E. and Grunig, L. (eds), *Public Relations Research Annual*, 1, 67–86.
5 The full version of the Johnson & Johnson Credo can be found at www.jnj.com/wps/wcm/connect/c7933f004f5563df9e22be1bb31559c7/jnj_ourcredo_english_us_8.5x11_cmyk.pdf?MOD=AJPERES.
6 Powell, M. (2011). Ethics and the public relations management process. In Moss, D. and DeSanto, B. (eds), *Public Relations: a Managerial Perspective*. London: Sage.

7   Jones, C., Parker, M. and ten Bos, R. (2005). *For Business Ethics*. Abingdon: Routledge.
8   Grunig, L.A. (2008). Using qualitative research to become the 'thinking heart' of organisations. In van Ruler, B., Tkalac Verčič, A. and Verčič, D. (eds), *Public Relations Metrics: Research and Evaluation*. New York: Routledge.
9   Van Riel, C.B.M. and Fombrun, C. (2007). *Essentials of Corporate Communication*. Abingdon: Routledge, p. 35.
10 The Arthur W. Page Society discusses authenticity in a public relations and communications context; see Arthur W. Page Society (2007). *The Authentic Enterprise*. Available at awpagesociety.com.
11 Bowen, S.A. (2010). The nature of good in public relations: what should be its normative ethic? In Heath, R.L. (ed.), *The Sage Handbook of Public Relations*. Thousand Oaks, CA: Sage.
12 Bernstein, D. (2009). Rhetoric and reputation: thoughts on corporate dissonance, *Management Decision*, 47(4), 603–615.
13 Stoker, K. and Rollins, B. (2010). Taking the BS out of PR: creating genuine messages by emphasising character and authenticity, *Ethical Space: The International Journal of Communication Ethics*. 7(2/3), 61–69.
14 Bowen, S.A. (2010). The nature of good in public relations: what should be its normative ethic? In Heath, R.L. (ed.), *The Sage Handbook of Public Relations*. Thousand Oaks, CA: Sage.
15 Ten universal absolutes are cited in Josephson, M. (1993). Teaching ethical decision making and principled reasoning, *Business Ethics*, annual edition 1993–1994. Guilford, CN: Daskin. Publishing Group. These are: honesty, integrity, promise keeping, fidelity, fairness, caring for others, respect for others, responsible citizenship, pursuit of excellence and accountability.
16 The non-cognitivist school of thought draws heavily on the work of Kenneth Burke and is represented in the public relations literature by rhetorical theorists such as Pearson; see Pearson, R. (1989). Business ethics as communication ethics: public relations practice and the idea of dialogue. In Botan, C.H. and Hazelton, V. (eds), *Public Relations Theory*. Mahwah, NJ: Lawrence Erlbaum Associates; Toth, E. and Heath, R.L. (1992). *Rhetorical and Critical Approaches to Public Relations*. London: Routledge; and Heath, R.L. (2010). Mind, self, and society. In Heath, R.L. (ed.), *The Sage Handbook of Public Relations*. Thousand Oaks, CA: Sage.
17 Habermas, J. (1984). *The Theory of Communicative Action, Vol. 1: Reason and the Rationalization of Society*, McCarthy, T. (trans.). Boston, MA: Beacon.
18 For a good explanation of Utilitarianism see Driver, J. (2007). *Ethics: The Fundamentals*. Malden, MA: Blackwell.
19 For a full version of the UN Declaration of Human Rights see www.un.org/overview/rights.html.
20 For a good explanation of Kant's philosophy and deontology see Driver, J. (2007). *Ethics* (see above).
21 Such as the universal absolutes identified by Josephson in note 15 above.
22 For a good explanation of virtue ethics see Driver, J. (2007). *Ethics* (see above).
23 Bowen, S.A. (2010). The nature of good in public relations: what should be its normative ethic? In Heath, R.L. (ed.), *The Sage Handbook of Public Relations*. Thousand Oaks, CA: Sage, p. 579.
24 Schein, L.K. (1985). *Organisational Culture and Leadership*. San Francisco: Jossey-Bass.
25 Rouleau, L. and Balogun, J. (2011). Middle managers, strategic sense making, and discursive competence, *Journal of Management Studies*, 48(3), 953–982.
26 Trevino, L.K., Brown, M. and Pincus-Hartman, L. (2003). A qualitative investigation of perceived executive ethical leadership: perceptions from inside and outside the executive suite, *Human Relations*, 56(1), 5–37.

27 Gregory, A. (2008) The competencies of senior practitioners in the UK: an initial study, *Public Relations Review*, 34(3), 215–23.
28 More can be read on moral courage in leaders in Cavanaugh, G.F. and Moberg, D.J. (1999). The virtue of courage within the organization. In Pava, M.L. and P. Primaux, P. (eds), *Research in Ethical Issues in Organisations*. Stamford, CT: JAI Press; Paine, L.S. (1999). Managing for organisational integrity. In Donaldson, T. and Werhane, P.H. (eds), *Ethical Issues in Business: A Philosophical Approach*, 6th edition. Upper Saddle River, NJ: Prentice Hall, pp. 526–38. Both cited in Bowen, S.A. (2010). The nature of good in public relations, p. 579 (see above).
29 The Seven Principles of Public Life are: selflessness (acting solely in the public interest); integrity (individual should not place themselves under any financial or other obligation which may unduly influence them); objectivity (in carrying out their public business); accountability (willing to submit themselves to any scrutiny appropriate to their office); openness (about their decisions and actions, given reasons and only restricting information when the wider public interest is at stake); honesty (declaring any private interests and resolving any resultant conflicts); and leadership (promoting and supporting the principles through leadership and example). For more information see www.public-standards.org.uk/About/The_7_Principles.html.
30 Edward Freeman is regarded as the first person to systematically expound stakeholder theory in his seminal book Freeman, R.E. (1984). *Strategic Management: A Stakeholder Approach*. Boston: Pitman.
31 Phillips, R. Freeman, E.R. and Wicks, A.C. (2003). What stakeholder theory is not, *Business Ethics Quarterly*, 13(4), 479– 502, p. 481.
32 This is how the South West Yorkshire NHS Partnership Trust explains values.
33 For the full version of the NHS Constitution see www.dh.gov.uk/prod_consum_dh/ groups/dh_digitalassets/@dh/@en/@ps/documents/digitalasset/dh_113645.pdf.
34 For further details see www.globalreporting.org/Pages/default.aspx.
35 For further details see www.theiirc.org/.
36 Pruzan, P. (1998). From control to values based management and accountability. *Journal of Business Ethics*, 17, 1379–94.
37 There are several authors who describe ethical decision-making models, for example Parsons, P. (2004). *Ethics in Public Relations*. London: Kogan Page; Powell, M. (2011). *Ethics and the Public Relations Management Process*. In Moss, D. and DeSanto, B. (eds), *Public Relations: a Managerial Perspective*. London: Sage; and Trevino, L.K. and K.A. Nelson (2004). *Managing Business Ethics*, 3rd edition. Hoboken, NJ: John Wiley & Sons.
38 Potter, R. (1972). The logic of moral argument. In Deats, P. (ed.), *Towards a Discipline of Social Ethics*. Boston: Boston University Press.

9   Enacting the role

Introduction

This chapter discusses how public relations leaders behave. It links to Chapter 5 which touched on the subject of roles, which will be developed more here. It also leads on from Chapter 3 on leadership. Our belief is that behaviours, along with skills and knowledge lie at the heart of professional credibility. Indeed, there is an argument that behaviours are even more important than knowledge and skills. We know quite senior leaders whose knowledge and skills appear flaky, but they certainly know how to behave and what language to use in senior circles.

Understanding the contribution public relations can make to the organisation, an ability to plan and make strategic interventions based on knowledge and skill, and having the requisite repertoire of behaviours are the three cornerstones of this book. The importance of behaviours cannot be overstated. Our phrase is 'enacting the role'.

The chapter covers three areas:

*   Organisational roles: how they are defined and the roles of senior public relations leaders; why these leaders are not as senior as they think they should be; what chief executive officers (CEOs) want from their public relations leaders; how respect is gained
*   Knowledge and skills: the basic toolkit
*   Behaviours: why they are important and the behavioural priorities

The roles people play

As mentioned in Chapter 5, roles are determined by the organisation; by what senior managers perceive they should be and the value they place on them. Ultimately it is the CEO and the board to determine who will be in the 'top team' and there is ample evidence that other 'C suite' executives take their cue from the CEO.[1]

Kim Harrison[2] cites four factors that affect the roles public relations leaders play:

*   'people' factor: the personal credibility and standing of professionals with senior management (more on this later);

- top management understanding and expectations of public relations (more on how this can be enhanced later);
- organisational and industry context: where an organisation operates in the fast-moving and highly competitive context, the value of public relations is normally appreciated more;
- the nature of the strategy-making process: public relations has to demonstrate its essential contribution to developing strategy and organisational outcomes, not just its ability to communicate strategy.

Turning to the individual, it would be a mistake to believe that successful public relations practitioners have a typical background and career path: there are many routes to the top.[3] It would also be a mistake to think that every professional has the requisite capabilities to reach the top.[4] To be a public relations leader requires a complex mix of knowledge, skills and abilities. These include *personal attributes and characteristics*, including professional experience, gender, personality and charisma, combined with the *organisational factors* mentioned above.[5] It is the amalgamation and enactment of these that leads to particular behaviours by individuals. Acceptable behaviours at work are not purely intuitive. Organisations have expectations about how individuals enact a particular role. Competencies are the behavioural repertoires or sets of behaviours that leaders are expected to perform so that the organisation can meet its objectives.[6] They are how knowledge and skills are used and applied and how personal attributes are enlisted to achieve the task.

While this chapter concentrates on behaviours, the book as a whole is about leadership. So, without covering the ground that Chapter 3 already has, a number of points have to be made to set the context for what follows:

- Leaders communicate their values in behaviour and the outcomes of those behaviours are crucially important.[7] They influence the culture of the organisation and the attitudes and priorities of those they lead (see also Chapter 8 on ethics).
- In a national survey of US public relations professionals,[8] two related positive leadership styles were found: transformational and inclusive. Transformational leaders inspire followers through communication, and inclusive leaders actively seek the participation of others. In combination the styles positively affect the strategy and outcomes of public relations.
- Characteristics of positive leaders include strong ethical orientation, vision, communication, decision-making skills, empathy and concern for organisational colleagues and other stakeholders.[9]
- 'Leadership requires a steady hand, good insights, inspiring vision and a superior understanding of the world.'[10]

With this in mind, it is appropriate to look at the roles senior communicators undertake which have been uncovered through extensive research over the last 30 years.

The earlier research,[11] drawing on the consulting literature, identified two major roles for practitioners:

- the *communication technician*: who does not make organisational decisions, but carries out public relations programmes in line with the instructions of others;
- the *communication manager*: who counsels management, makes communication policy, and manages public relations programmes.

Within this manager category, there are three main types of role. The *expert prescriber*, who researches and defines public relations problems, develops programmes and implements them, sometimes with the assistance of others. The *communication facilitator,* who acts as a liaison person, facilitating two-way communication between the organisation and its stakeholders. This person acts as interpreter and mediator. The *problem-solving process facilitator*, who helps others in the organisation solve their communication problems. This person acts as a counsellor/adviser on the planning and implementation of programmes. It is a role often fulfilled by specialist consultancies. Researchers also identified a 'senior adviser' role at the senior level: someone who acts as a high-level counsellor, constantly advising the CEO or chair of the board. They have a wide ranging remit, but are essentially charged with spotting issues for the individual with whom they work and advising them on how to respond.

Scandinavian researchers[12] discovered three key roles for senior public relations executives. The first is as *organisational leader* who has responsibility with other senior managers for all strategic decisions. Second, the *communication leader* whose responsibility covers communication strategy and issues. And finally, the *communication manager* who is responsible for communication, but is not a member of the senior management group.

A European study of public relations roles[13] points to four characteristics which defines the contribution that professionals make to organisations. These are given in Table 9.1.

Work undertaken in the UK and US by Danny Moss and colleagues[14] isolated five elements to the communication/public relations manager role. One was undertaking high-level technical work, with the other four managerial roles being:

- *monitor and evaluator*: describes the responsibilities that practitioners have for organising, controlling and monitoring the work of their departments both internally and externally;
- *key policy and strategy adviser*: concerns the relationship senior practitioners should have with their senior management although the researchers found that this was more of an expectation than a reality;
- *issues management expert*: here the practitioner's role is identifying and responding to external threats and interpreting them;

Table 9.1 The four characteristics of European communication/public relations

REFLECTIVE	MANAGERIAL
Analysing changing standards, values and standpoints in society and discussing these with members of the organisation in order to adjust the standard, values/standpoint of the organisation accordingly. Concerned with organisational standards, values and views and aimed at the development of mission and organisational standards.	Developing plans to communicate and maintain relationships with public groups in order to gain public trust and/or mutual understanding. Concerned with commercial and other (internal and external) public groups and with public opinion as a whole, and is aimed at the execution of the organisation's mission and strategies.
OPERATIONAL	EDUCATIONAL
Preparing the means of communication for the organisation (and its members) in order to help the organisation formulate its communications. Concerned with services and aimed at implementation of communication plans developed by others.	Helping all members of the organisation to become communicatively competent in order to respond to societal demands. Concerned with the thinking and behaviour of organisational members and aimed at internal publics.

- *troubleshooting/problem solver*: this relates to the practitioner reacting to and dealing with internal and external challenges, threats and crises, and they are recognised as the person nominated to do so. The difference between this and issues management is that whereas the former is a predictive and advisory role, this latter role is focused on the day-to-day operational.

The fact that there are so many articulations of the roles of senior public relations practitioners indicates a challenge. Their roles are extremely broad and variable, highly dependent on the specific contexts and difficult to describe. Given this, it is hard to gain clarity on even the levels of skills and knowledge that are required to underpin these roles, let alone describe the behaviours needed to enact them.

A good starting point, however, given the roles are defined by senior managers and especially the CEO, is to look acts the expectations and they have. This was alluded to briefly in Chapter 5, but is explored more thoroughly here. There have been several studies[15] on what CEOs require from their senior practitioners. Drawing these together yields the following list:

- detailed knowledge of the business;
- detailed knowledge of the external environment;
- extensive internal networks and relationships;
- a broad and varied public relations background;
- credibility with senior managers;
- a team player;
- an educator and coach;
- an individual on top of the issues and able to advise on them;
- an ability to engage in multiple stakeholder relationships with a mature and long-term perspective (authentic rather than purely transactional);

- a strong ethical base and personal integrity;
- an individual who will tell the CEO 'how it is' and provide honest feedback from stakeholders;
- good understanding of the brand and an ability to promote and defend it;
- an ability to develop both business and public relations strategies.

Before moving on to what successful public relations leaders do in detail, it is worth considering briefly two issues that constantly arise in discussions that we have with senior practitioners. The first is why public relations is not valued as much as it should be, and, second, how that can be rectified.

First the good news. There are a number of surveys[16] asking where the most senior public relations professional is located in the organisational hierarchy, and although the figures provide inconsistent results, it is clear that the trend is upward with more having board positions and about 50 per cent of those surveyed now reporting to the CEO, chair or chief operating officer. So what is preventing the other half of senior communicators progressing to these heights? The problem is largely with public relations people themselves and the solution is largely in their hands. While there is still some prejudice against public relations as a discipline, most CEOs and chairs interviewed in the studies indicated earlier do understand its importance and wish to employ very senior and skilled practitioners. Their problem is that they find it difficult to recruit individuals with the right capabilities. The main issues are:

- a lack of broad industry and general business knowledge which is required in all board level directors, including legal, financial and strategic understanding and capability;[17]
- an inability or lack of experience in dealing with organisational politics and power relations;[18]
- over-reliance on technical skills such as how to handle social media, run complex events and liaise with stakeholders – financial directors rarely talk about the technicalities of the balance sheet although they can do in detail when required to;
- gaps in knowledge in their own subject, for example being able to explain the science of public relations rather than relying on experience;[19]
- gaps in general business capabilities such as leadership and coaching, an ability to work at all levels and general networking skills;[20]
- a lack of some personal attributes, for example self-insight, assertiveness, an ability to make difficult decisions, confidence, flexibility and energy.[21]

It is apparent therefore that addressing these issues will begin to position senior public relations professionals for higher level roles, but there are four other factors that gain respect and organisational influence.

The first is excellent performance in the current role and that includes technical proficiency (see Chapter 12). Promotion is often based on personal credibility and senior managers' confidence that a contribution can be made at a higher level.

Second, it is vital to attach to the CEO's agenda. CEOs appreciate problem solvers and proactive managers who provide solutions to the issues they are dealing with.

Third, board-level aspirants have to hone their influencing skills[22] and use them astutely. Taking opportunities to influence and potentially change senior managers' opinions of the role by demonstrating value and an ability to contribute more widely is not just self-serving; it will be seen to benefit the whole organisation. There is nothing unethical about being influential. Linked to this point is that it is essential to learn the organisational language and behaviours. Senior managers, like all other groups, have their own recurring themes and vocabulary and ways of behaving; a familiarity with this ensures there is no barrier into strategic conversations and joining the group. A note of caution here though – mirroring language and behaviours uncritically is potentially dangerous. The public relations leader has to maintain something of the 'outsider' to retain objectivity and to discharge their ethical guardian and activist responsibilities (more on this in Chapter 11).

The fourth factor is to learn the skill of being a trusted adviser, an adept internal consultant. David Nadler[23] has written extensively on this from an external adviser point of view, but there are many lessons for the internal adviser. These include understanding what it is like to be a CEO in today's challenging environment, the importance of listening, the ability to synthesise information, to summarise problems succinctly and provide viable options. This is solid advice and has skills, knowledge and behaviour at its heart.

While it is quite legitimate for senior practitioners to aspire to be at the board table, or a formal member of the decision-making elite – the dominant coalition – it is not necessary to have this position to be of such importance.[24] The senior adviser role mentioned earlier is a powerful and influential position. The crucial issues are ready access to the elite, credibility, assurance that the public relations leader's opinion counts and that the public relations contribution is championed by an informed senior manager when decisions are made. A useful personal exercise is for leaders to analyse who they spend time with, what the nature of the interactions are and whether the agendas of senior people are being addressed through these interactions.

Given that competencies or behavioural repertoires are knowledge and skills in action it is now worth summarising these before focusing on behaviours.

The knowledge and skills set of senior communicators

It is helpful here to provide a definition of terms: *knowledge* is what practitioners need to *know* in order to undertake their role competently; *skills* are what practitioners need to be able to *do* to undertake their role competently.

There are different approaches to identifying knowledge and skills. An interesting take on this is that of the Swedish Public Relations Association.[25] Its research identified four areas where the practitioner needs to develop knowledge:

- *Processes* create working reality and communicate. Practitioners need to know about organisational design because this creates both opportunities and weaknesses which in turn create communication issues.
- *Structure* includes both physical and mental elements and transparency in both is needed if a holistic view of the organisation is to be communicated.
- *Social interaction* of people in the organisation can be either negative and used as a basis for power plays, or positive with free knowledge sharing, but both affect communicative ability.
- *Organisation-wide relationships* refers to the relationships the organisation has with others in its environment, clearly important for communications.

There are also four skills related to these areas of knowledge (for more on this see also Chapter 11):

- *System designer*: the senior practitioner needs to be involved in processes and structures, to facilitate good communication flows which are organisational enablers.
- *Mediator:* not primarily to defuse potential conflicts, but to create shared understandings and perceptions or 'meaning' within the organisation, a highly skilled and varied contribution.
- *Coach:* to develop the communication skills of others.
- *Influencer*: facilitating conceptual changes in the minds of those in the organisation. This is profoundly bound up in the development of organisational culture. Of course there are deep ethical implications in this role.

The more typical inventories list the main areas of work undertaken by practitioners along with the knowledge and skills needed to underpin these. Many professional associations have such matrices[26] and organisations such as the Universal Accreditation Board (UAP) and International Association of Business Communicators (IABC) have transnational accreditation schemes which also describe required knowledge, skills and abilities. Most of these frameworks have a combination of what are called domain specific (i.e. pertaining specifically to public relations) and general business knowledge and skills[27] and often break them into levels depending on the seniority of the practitioner.[28] The enhanced UAB[29] list shown in Table 9.2 provides 12 common work categories and 10 associated knowledge, skills and ability areas.

How knowledge, skills and abilities are used in performance comprises the set of behaviours or competencies practitioners enact, and it is to this that the chapter now turns.

Table 9.2 The UAB work categories and knowledge, skills and abilities which underpin practitioner competence

Work categories	
Account/client management	Strategic planning
Public relations programme planning	Project management
Media relations	Social media relations
Stakeholder relations	Issues management
Crisis management	Internal relations and employee communications
Special events, conferences and meetings	Community relations

Knowledge, skills and abilities	
Researching, planning, implementing and evaluating programmes	Ethics and law
Communication models and theories	Business literacy
Management skills and issues	Crisis communication management
Media relations	Using information technology efficiently
History of and current issues in public relations	Advanced communication skills

The behaviours of public relations leaders

The research underpinning the behavioural work now outlined was funded by the UK Department of Health and became part of the larger project which generated the model outlined in Chapter 5.[30] It is the first systematic study[31] of behaviours in public relations and was undertaken by trained occupational psychologists using a globally validated method[32] in a research project directed by one of us. The research investigated board-level communicators in the public and private sectors to discover if they had a specific and identifiable set of behaviours and whether there were differences between the sectors.

The methodology used produces a unique set of competencies for each group it is applied to and the results given in Tables 9.3 and 9.4 are an aggregate for the private and public sectors respectively. Hence, each individual in the group displays all the behaviours, but the balance of behaviours differs from individual to individual and is dependent on the situations they face. The order in which they are presented is not prioritised.

The research confirms and adds to the conclusions of some of the earlier studies. Senior practitioners based in the private sector in particular fulfil the

Table 9.3 The ten competency titles, descriptions and behavioural indicators for private-sector communicators

Strategic/Long-term View	Leading and Supporting	Making Decisions and Acting	Maintaining a Positive Outlook	Networking
Thinks broadly and strategically. Plans ahead and remains focused on organisational objectives.	Provides direction, advice and coaching to individuals or teams. Supports and encourages others. Fosters openness and information sharing.	Willing to make tough decisions quickly based on the information available. Successfully generates activity and shows confidence in the chosen course of action.	Responds positively to changes or setbacks. Remains calm and in control of own emotions, manages pressure well.	Talks easily to people at all levels both internally and externally. Canvases opinions widely and builds strong infrastructures to receive and disseminate information.
• Develops an agreed understanding of key business issues • Evaluates actions in terms of their potential impact on overall organisational objectives • Thinks ahead and focuses on the future rather than the past • Shows awareness of long-term benefits over short-term political issues • Maintains a vision of objectives and regularly reviews those objectives • Thinks broadly beyond immediate issues • Shows recognition of impact on the bottom line • Keeps up to date with market and competitor developments • Considers links between seemingly unrelated issues	• Provides others with a clear direction • Elevates insights to the board • Builds a strong team of talented individuals • Gives advice and coaches others • Demonstrates commitment to the development of staff • Delegates work appropriately to others • Offers challenging opportunities to staff • Acknowledges the contribution of others through formal or informal recognition • Maintains confidences • Creates an open culture of information sharing	• Weighs up the positive and negative outcomes of a decision • Makes tough decisions • Identifies urgent decisions • Makes unpopular decisions • Suggests various courses of action • Decides upon a course of action quickly • Takes calculated risks on the basis of adequate analysis • Uses facts and figures when making decisions • Acts with confidence when executing decisions • Makes things happen • Implements solutions	• Looks for positive outcomes and remains optimistic • Communicates messages of hope • Uses humour • Shows awareness of the differences between setback and failure • Deals with ambiguity, making positive use of the opportunities it presents • Keeps emotions under control during difficult situations • Works productively in a pressurised environment • Remains buoyant in emotional or difficult situations • Remains emotionally stable in challenging circumstances	• Seeks opportunities to interact with people at all levels • Builds relationships with 'gatekeepers' • Consults with subject-matter experts • Talks to people regularly • Canvases suggestions and options • Builds relationships across functions • Seeks to build relationships with key individuals • Builds relationships externally • Develops an extended network via team • Imparts knowledge and expertise to others • Makes themselves visible throughout organisation

continued...

Table 9.3 continued

Communicating	Investigating and analysing	Taking Responsibility for High Standards	Preparing Thoroughly	Understanding Others
Communicates verbally and in writing clearly, consistently and convincingly both internally and externally.	Gathers, probes and tests information. Shows evidence of clear analytical thinking. Gets to the heart of complex problems and issues.	Behaves consistently with clear personal values that support those of the organisation. Takes responsibility for the standard of organisational communication and for their own and team's actions	Spends time understanding tasks and objectives. Prepares carefully and thoroughly for situations that may occur and cause difficulties. Prepares for formal events and meetings.	Remains open minded when taking into account individual views and needs. Demonstrates interest in others and is empathetic to their concerns. Works towards solutions of mutual benefit.
• Communicates clearly and concisely to all interested parties • Sends a consistent message to all • Adapts communication to the needs of the audience • Uses probing questions to challenge views • Speaks with conviction • Support arguments with facts and figures • Articulates the reasons behind actions • Communicates internally in an open and direct way • Confronts senior people with difficult issues • Clarifies that a shared understanding has been received • Writes clearly and engagingly • Make use of contemporary channels of communication	• Gathers information from a wide variety of source • Seeks out different situations to find new information • Uses personal experience to help understand problems • Probes for further information to clarify vague or confusing issues • Breaks information into component parts and relationships • Distinguishes the core issues from peripheral issues of a situation • Identifies similarities between situations • Rapidly grasps the key facts of a situation • Identifies and highlights key facts and figures • Uses numbers and statistics when analysing information • Analyses the potential outcomes of a situation	• Sets high goals and standards • Behaves consistently in line with organisational values • Clearly defines boundaries for information sharing • Takes responsibility for the team's actions • Accepts that mistakes are made • Admits own mistakes • Handles criticism well and learns from it • Acts quickly to overcome errors • Seeks help from others when required • Stops communication if necessary	• Plans how objectives can be achieved • Involves team in planning process • Develops plans that take account of potential changing or difficult circumstances • Monitors situations carefully • Maintains a constant awareness of issues helping or hindering progress • Prepares thoroughly for meetings and interviews • Rehearses arguments • Writes agendas	• Understands the objectives of all parties • Works towards a win-win situation • Asks questions around individual's own issues • Works to understand the motivations of others • Keeps an open mind when others are expressing their views • Tolerates differing needs and viewpoints • Picks up on verbal/non-verbal cues • Considers the impact of action on other people • Shows respect and sensitivity to individual needs and cultural differences • Shows an interest in people • Responds with sympathy

senior adviser role.[33] It is also apparent that for all senior practitioners technical implementation roles cannot be escaped.

Turning to the private-sector group, the evidence indicates that the *understanding others* behaviour is slightly more prominent than others. This competency not only involves understanding the views of those inside and outside the organisation, but a profound understanding of their motivations and aspirations. This is important in determining the requirements for and the contents of public relations programmes. These senior practitioners are able to form a holistic view of all the different points of view expressed and are able to negotiate positions to develop win-win solutions.

The *strategic/long-term view* competency has special relevance to commercial, 'bottom line' impacts. This competency relates closely to the *investigating and analysing*, and *preparing thoroughly* and *making decisions and acting* competencies. These are linked to a good understanding of the industry, the business and business strategy. They underline an ability to handle, use and interpret information and business intelligence and a willingness to take tough, evidence-based decisions which lead to decisive actions. These competencies clearly demonstrate the abilities deemed essential by chief executives.

Other competencies worth special mention are *taking responsibility for high standards*, with its implications of personal values and ethics, and *maintaining a positive outlook*, with its links to personal attributes such as positivity, flexibility and remaining calm under pressure. Deeper questioning in this area revealed that senior communicators were very aware that their behaviour at times of crisis and extreme pressure was of great organisational value and gained them significant professional credibility.

In the public sector, the *building strong relations* and *consulting and involving* competencies were regarded as more important. It is certainly the case that government demands consultation by many public-sector organisations, but this commitment goes beyond these requirements. A feature of those practitioners working in the public sector is that they are not primarily motivated by power or a desire to make money. They are in the service because they want to make a difference to society. This commitment is very strong and permeates thinking and behaviour. The desire to 'build community' infuses much of their day-to-day activity.

Slightly behind these two competencies came *taking action* and *upholding the reputation of the service*. These leaders frequently work in localities where there are contested issues and many divergent and opposing viewpoints. They are clear and transparent in decision-making and a defined ethical framework guides the decisions they take, with duty to the public being a displayed value. The heavy emphasis on 'people' is noticeable and this demands collaborative, consensual working both internally (with political as well as officer colleagues) and externally. Skilled persuasion and delicate, sensitive mediation involving negotiated positions between stakeholders is an essential requirement of the role.

Table 9.4 The ten competency titles, descriptions and behavioural indicators for public-sector communicators

Understanding the bigger picture Demonstrates a comprehensive understanding of the impact of organisational strategy on own responsibilities.	*Taking Action* Makes prompt and clear decisions, empowers others to do the same.	*Consulting and Involving* Works with staff, patients and the wider community to ensure successful consultation and support.	*Presenting and Communicating* Ensures audience understanding through the use of an appropriate and interactive communication style.	*Creating and Innovating*
• Understands how organisational strategies relate to the bigger picture • Considers the impact of organisational strategies on others • Ensures plans are aligned to organisational development • Puts communication at the heart of organisational development • Prioritises resources and projects according to organisational needs • Recognises when it is appropriate to alter plans when strategies change • Takes account of a wide range of issues across, and related to, the organisation • Understands the pros and cons of a solution	• Makes prompt and clear decisions when dealing with contentious issues • Takes responsibility for people and projects • Delivers on promises • Involves relevant people in the decision-making process • Empowers others to make decisions where appropriate • Escalates issues when necessary • Takes initiative and works under own direction • Gives direction to the decision-making of others	• Listens to the views of others • Encourages others to contribute • Encourages effective team-working • Brings people with the right skills into a project • Shows an awareness of the diverse views of others • Works with people to build acceptable solutions • Develops the skill of individuals and teams • Consults and involves others to gain their support	• Communicates clearly and succinctly, both orally and in writing • Translates complex messages into communication that is relevant for the audience • Adapts communication style according to individual needs • Develops communication that meet the requirements of the particular situation • Projects credibility when presenting information to others • Provides others with the information they need to present a convincing case • Finds new ways to present information to maintain the interest of the audience • Uses an open and interactive communication style	• Finds ways to innovate • Looks for new solutions to old problems • Seeks out opportunities to change things • Looks for alternatives • Introduces change sensitively, but firmly

Formulating Strategies and Concepts	Managing Under Pressure	Building Strong Relationships	Upholding the reputation of the Service	Persuading and Influencing
Finds ways to enable self and others to cope with difficult challenges, demonstrates clear thinking and keeps problems in perspective.	Relates well to a broad range of people, building and maintaining an extensive network of contacts.	Behaves consistently with clear personal values which complement those of the organisation and wider community.	Gains clear agreement and commitment to an agreed course of action through effective persuasion and negotiation.	
• Thinks broadly • Able to identify the important organisational imperatives • Approaches work strategically • Sets and develops communications strategy • Establishes a vision for the communication department • Is able to conceptualise difficult issues clearly and come up with solutions	• Keeps emotions under control in difficult times • Balances the demands of work and personal life • Finds ways to cope with the pressure and expectations that they face • Draws on personal experiences to help self and others through difficult situations • Keeps difficult challenges in perspective • Copes with a changing environment and helps others to feel comfortable with it • Demonstrates clear and realistic thinking when faced with difficult issues • Focuses energy on the most important and relevant issues	• Builds rapport quickly and makes people feel at ease • Establishes strong relationships with people from all backgrounds • Establishes strong working relationships with people at all levels of the organisation • Builds and maintains strong people networks • Knows who to speak to when particular information is required • Gathers perceptions to increase understanding of underlying organisational issues • Uses humour appropriately to build relationships • Creates a safe environment that encourages others to share information with them	• Upholds the ethics and values of the service • Demonstrates integrity by acting openly and honestly • Promotes and defends equal opportunities • Builds diverse teams that reflect the wider community • Deals sensitively with personal information • Takes pride in delivering a service to the community • Gains the respect and trust of others • Gives honest and objective advice to others	• Persuades others to agree course of action • Helps others to understand different viewpoints and find common ground • Guides conversations to a desired endpoint • Manages conflict sensitively and diplomatically • Makes a strong personal impression on others • Influences the agendas of others • Takes account of the internal and external political climate when persuading others • Closes discussion with clear commitment to action from both sides

Comparing the private and public sectors shows a great deal of commonality in behaviours, but also shows some differences. The comparisons are summarised in Table 9.5.

A number of the competencies can be seen to be almost directly equivalent and are paired at the top of Table 9.5. The *leading and supporting* and *understanding others* competencies from the private sector and *consulting and involving* from the public sector are overlapping. However, there is a slightly different emphasis in each. For the public sector the competency focuses on the importance of consultation and involvement with the community, whereas for the private sector, this was found to be more internally focused. Again, this can be partly explained by the driving purpose of public-sector work, building and working with communities, whereas for the private sector this was focused on engaging internal colleagues in the pursuit of organisational objectives. *Taking responsibility for high standards* in the private sector and *upholding the reputation of the service* in the public sector can also be seen to be similar. For the private sector the emphasis was on the personal standards of the senior communicator, whereas for the public sector the ethics and conduct of the whole organisation to perform for the public good was the concern. A possible explanation here is that private-sector public relations leaders may regard themselves as exemplars of ethical standards within their organisations and this lends credibility to their role as the 'ethical guardian' for the whole organisation.

Table 9.5 A comparison of private- and public-sector competencies

Private Sector	Public Sector
Strategic/Long-term View	Understanding the Bigger Picture
Leading and Supporting Understanding others	Consulting and Involving
Maintaining a Positive Outlook	Managing Under Pressure
Taking Responsibility for High Standards	Upholding the Reputation of the Service
Communicating	Presenting and Communicating
Making Decisions and Acting	Taking Action
Networking	Building Strong Relationships
Investigating and Analysing	
Preparing Thoroughly	
	Formulating Strategies and Concepts
	Persuading and Influencing
	Creating and Innovating

There are some competencies in the private sector which are not apparent in the public sector and vice versa. *Investigating and analysing* does not appear in the public sector list. This could be because this type of work is completed by less senior colleagues or by specialist departments in the public sector. In addition, public relations leaders in the public sector appear to be more involved in technical implementation work with a significant amount being reactive, especially media relations. This may mean they have less time for considered investigation and analysis. On the other hand, the market imperatives of the private sector and a competitive external environment require constant updating and analysis of information. A more turbulent environment requires more proactive external analysis. That is not to say that turbulence is not a factor in the public sector, but it is of a different nature, often driven by political rather than market imperatives with the required change being to clear and fixed ends. Thus, environmental analysis for external change is not required as much in the public sector.

The absence of the *preparing thoroughly* competence in the public sector is rather more difficult to explain. Close scrutiny revealed that public-sector professionals appear to be under more work pressure than their private-sector colleagues and it could well be that public-sector professionals simply do not have the time to devote to careful preparation and have no support to delegate these activities too.

The *persuading and influencing* competence is not as pronounced in the private sector. This reinforces the emerging picture that gaining commitment by influencing others is a critical behaviour in the public sector. The task of building consensus particularly when there are political overlays is a complex and difficult task requiring immense skill and particular behaviours.

It is perhaps surprising given that private-sector practitioners plan extensively that the *formulating strategies and concepts* competence is absent in their behaviour set. However, this relates more to formulating operational plans and campaigns and reflects the high level of operational work public-sector practitioners are involved in and the sometimes bureaucratic approvals processes they have to go through. It is also a source of frustration in the public sector because practitioners felt they are capable of being involved in strategic planning at a higher level as policies were being formulated, but are often restricted to tactical implementation.

Finally, the *creating and innovating* competence is present only in the public sector and can be explained by the fact that operational campaigns in the public sector usually have very restricted budgets and are often about long-term social change. Therefore, creativity and innovation in maximising the impact of those campaigns over a sustained period is a stock in trade of the job. While this is true of the private sector too, on the whole this requirement is more apparent in the public sector.

Overall, these results show a great deal of similarity between the private and public sectors with the main points of difference reducing to two areas. First, the more overt business-oriented behaviours of analysis and investigation, thinking strategically and preparation are more observable in the private sector where a focus on business performance is important. Collaboration, cooperation and involvement characterise the behaviours of those involved in public-sector work and this is driven by an emphasis on societal concerns and a requirement for democratic and transparent working with stakeholders.

Finally, it is important to emphasise that competencies are behaviours required to achieve particular organisational objectives and these will differ from industry to industry and sector to sector. The competencies indicated above are not necessarily the behaviours of those individuals in their private lives or the behaviours they would display for another employer, organisation or sector.

Summary

What this chapter has sought to demonstrate is that having superior knowledge and consummate skill is not enough to be a public relations leader. Yet the authors have found that even with senior practitioners there is a naive belief that this will suffice and frustration that their careers are not advancing. Serious consideration about how the senior leaders' role is enacted has to be undertaken along with learning of the behavioural repertoires that characterise leaders in the most senior positions in organisations. It is salutary to reflect that there are senior individuals in every organisation whose skill and knowledge is in doubt, but they have a profound understanding of how to enact a role, and it is this rather that other attributes which has gained them their position in the organisation.

Notes

1 See Gregory, A. and Edwards, L. (2004). *Patterns of PR in Britain's 'Most Admired' Companies*. Report commissioned by Eloqui Public Relations from Leeds Business School, and Sterne, G.D. (2008). Business perceptions of public relations in New Zealand, *Journal of Communication Management*, 12(1), 30–50.
2 Harrison, K. (2011). *Strategic Public Relations: A Practical Guide to Success*. South Yarra: Palgrave Macmillan.
3 See research by Gregory, A. (2008). The competencies of senior practitioners in the UK: an initial study, *Public Relations Review*, 34(3), 215–223; Meng, J., Berger, B.K. and Heyman, W.C (2011). Measuring public relations leadership in the trait approach: a second-order factor model in the dimensional of self-dynamics, *Public Relations Journal*, 5(1), 1–20.
4 Berger, B.K., Meng, J. and Heyman, W.C (2009). Role modelling in public relations: the influence of role models and mentor is on leadership beliefs and qualities. Paper given at 12th international public relations research conference, Miami, FL. March.
5 Moss, D. and DeSanto, B. (2011). *Public Relations: A Managerial Perspective*. Los Angeles, CA: Sage.
6 Bartram, D. (2004), The SHL Competency Framework, SHL Business Series No. 4, Thames Ditton.
7 Schein, L.K. (1985). *Organisational Culture and Leadership*. San Francisco: Jossey-Bass.
8 Werder, K.P. and Holtzhausen, D. (2009). An analysis of the influence of public relations department leadership style on public relations strategy use and effectiveness. *Journal of Public Relations Research*, 21(4), 404–27.

9 Berger, B.K., Meng, J. and Heyman, W.C. (2009). Measuring public relations leadership in the trait approach: a second-order factor model in the dimensional of self-dynamics. *Public Relations Journal*, 5(1), 1–20.

10 Berger, B.K., Meng, J. and Heyman, W.C. (2009). Measuring public relations leadership in the trait approach, p. 20 (see above).

11 The earlier work on roles is well summarised in a paper by Dozier, D.M. and Broom, G.M. (1995). Evolution of the manager role in public relations practice. *Journal of Public Relations Research*, 7(1), 3–26.

12 Johansson, C. and Ottestig, A.T. (2011). Communication executives in a changing world: legitimacy beyond organizational borders. *Journal of Communication Management*, 15(2), 144–64.

13 Van Ruler, B., Verčič, D., Butschi, G. and Flodin, B. (2004). A first look for parameters of public relations in Europe, *Journal of Public Relations Research*. 16(1), 35–63.

14 For Moss and colleagues' work refer to Moss, D.A., Newman, A. and DeSanto, B. (2005). What do communications managers do? Defining and refining the core elements of management in a public relations/communication context, *Journalism and Mass Communication Quarterly*, 82, 873–90; DeSanto, B. and Moss, D.A. (2004). Rediscovering what PR managers do: rethinking the measurement of managerial behavior in the public relations context, *Journal of Communication Management*, 9(2), 179–96; Moss, D.A. and Green, R. (2001). Re-examining the manager's role in public relations: what management and public relations research teaches us, *Journal of Communications Management*, 6(2), 118–32; Moss, D.A., Warnaby, G. and Newman, A. (2000). Public relations practitioner role enactment at the senior management level within UK companies, *Journal of Public Relations Research*, 12(4), 277–307.

15 For example Arthur W. Page Society (2007). The Authentic Enterprise available from http://www.awpagesociety.com/insights/authentic-enterprise-report/; Murray, K. and White, J. (2005). CEO's views on reputation management, *Journal of Communication Management*, 9(4), 348–58; O'Neill, S.J. (2008) *World Class Communications: The View from Primary Care Trust Chief Executives*. Report for Centre of Public Relations Studies. Birmingham: Multi Communications; Sterne, G.D. (2008). Business perceptions of public relations in New Zealand, *Journal of communication Management*, 12(1), 30–50; Wells, T. (2009). *The Chief Executive, Communication and Engagement: An Attitudinal Survey of NHS Chief Executives in Yorkshire and Humber*. Report for Centre for Public Relations Studies. Spreyton: Gyroscope Consultancy.

16 For example, the Generally Accepted Practices (GAP) survey conducted by the USC Annenberg Strategic Communication and Public Relations Center, The European Communications Monitor, and the national professional associations such as the Public Relations Society of America, The Chartered Institute of Public Relations, the Public Relations Institute if New Zealand and the Public Relations Institute of South Africa

17 Reported by Berger, B.K., Meng, J. and Heyman, W.C. (2009). Role modelling in public relations (see above); Hogg, G. and Doolan, D. (1999). Playing the part: practitioner roles in public relations, *European Journal of Marketing*, 33 (5/6), 597–611; Moss, D.A., Newman, A. and DeSanto, B. (2005). What do communications managers do? Defining and refining the core elements of management in a public relations/communication context, *Journalism and Mass Communication Quarterly*, 8, 873–90.

18 Berger, B.K. and Reber, B.H. (2006). *Gaining Influence in Public Relations: The Role of Resistance in Practice*. Mahwah, NJ: Lawrence Erlbaum Associates.

19 Berger, B.K. and Meng, J. (2010). Public relations practitioners and the leadership challenge. In Heath, R.L. (ed.) *The Sage Handbook of Public Relations*. Los Angeles, CA: Sage, pp 421–34.

20 Johansson, C. and Ottestig, A.T. (2011). Communication executives in a changing world: legitimacy beyond organizational borders, *Journal of Communication Management*, 15(2), 144–64.
21 Harrison, K. (2011). *Strategic Public Relations: A Practical Guide to Success*. South Yarra: Palgrave Macmillan. Choi, Y. and Choi, J. (2009). Behavioural dimensions of public relations leadership in organizations, *Journal of Communication Management*, 13(2), 292–309. Jeffrey, L. and Brunton, M. (2010). Identifying competencies for communication practice: A needs assessment for curriculum development and selection in New Zealand. *Public Relations Review*, 36(2), 202–5.
22 See Harrison, K. (2011). *Strategic public relations*, Chapter 5 (see above) for a good summary of influencing skills.
23 For a summary of his approach see Nadler, D.A. (2005). Confessions of a trusted counselor, *Harvard Business Review*, 83(9), 68–77.
24 Johansson, C. and Ottestig, A.T. (2011). Communication executives in a changing world: legitimacy beyond organizational borders, *Journal of Communication Management*, 15(2), 144–64.
25 Hamrefors, S. (2010). Communicative leadership, *Journal of Communication Management*, 14(2), 141–52.
26 For example the Public Relations Society of America uses the Universal Accreditation Board; see www.praccreditation.org/becomeapr/ksas_competencies.html?utm_source=comprehension_blog&utm_medium=blog_post&utm_campaign=aprframework.
27 Jeffrey, L. and Brunton, M. (2010). Identifying competencies for communication practice: a needs assessment for curriculum development and selection in New Zealand, *Public Relations Review*, 36(2), 202–5.
28 See the Canadian Public Relations Society approach at www.cprs.ca/uploads/education/PathwaytoProfessionEng_Final_11-07-2011.pdf.
29 This enhanced UAB list was taken from Sha, B.-L. (2011) Does accreditation really matter in public relations practice? How age and experience compare to accreditation, *Public Relations Review*, 37(1), 1–11.
30 NHS (2009) *The Communicating Organisation: Using Communication to Support the Development of High-performing Organisations*. London: NHS. Available at www.dh.gov.uk/prod_consum_dh/groups/dh_digitalassets/documents/digitalasset/dh_110342.pdf
31 Gregory, A. (2008). The competencies of senior practitioners in the UK: an initial study, *Public Relations Review*, 34(3), 215–23.
32 Bartram, D. (2005), The great eight competencies: a criterion-centric approach to validation, *Journal of Applied Psychology*, 90(6), 1185–1203.
33 See Dozier, D.M. and Broom, G.M. (1995). Evolution of the manager role in public relations practice. *Journal of Public Relations Research*, (1), 3–26; Toth, E.L., Serini, S.A., Wright, D.K. and Emig, A.G. (1998). Trends in public relations roles: 1990–1995, *Public Relations Review*, 24(2), 145–63; and Moss, D.A. and Green, R. (2001). Re-examining the manager's role in public relations: what management and public relations research teaches us, *Journal of Communication Management*, 6(2), 118–32.

Part III

The responsibilities of public relations leaders

In this final part of the book we look at the specific responsibilities of public relations leaders, responsibilities in which they excel. Parts I and II looked at the strategic contribution of public relations and the preoccupations of the public relations leader. This has to be complemented by focusing on how these leaders discharge their public relations responsibilities on a daily basis.

We start with the most fundamental of responsibilities: that of planning public relations campaigns in a strategic way. This takes full account of the context in which planning takes place and the different levels within the organisation at which it applies. Two specific planning models are outlined and some of the most problematic areas discussed: these include setting effective objectives and evaluation. Our experience has shown that although it is a basic building block, knowledge of the principles of planning are still lacking in many public relations departments. Public relations leaders know that unless this fundamental business discipline is grasped and demonstrated, credibility is put in jeopardy.

Chapter 11 looks at the public relations as catalyst. It stresses that public relations is not just about building relationships, reputation and communicating, but that the public relations leader is involved in all aspects of organisational life including its structures, processes and systems. The whole organisation in all its aspects tells a story. The role of the public relations leader is to identify where the 'reality needs fixing' to reflect the aspirations and values which are being espoused.

When public relations practitioners get promoted, they often express a desire to move away from the technical aspects of the job. However, Chapter 12 makes a case for the public relations leader being an expert technician. Expertise is something that is gained with experience and therefore the expert technician's contribution is rather different from that of less senior colleagues. Expertise builds personal authority and gains the confidence of others.

In the modern world it is impossible and most likely undesirable for public relations to be the organisational gatekeeper. A key task therefore, is building communicative competence throughout the whole organisation. Just as the finance department and the human resources (HR) department have successfully 'off shored' budgeting and aspects of recruitment and staff discipline, the public relations function can take advantage of the willingness and capability of staff throughout the organisation to take on communication activities on behalf of the organisation. This of course includes those operating at the most senior level of the organisation who look to public relations to coach and mentor them. The key issue here is to build capability and Chapter 13 explores the role of the public relations leader as internal educator.

Part III finishes by focusing on the public relations leader as consultant, whether they work in-house or in a formal consultancy role. If others within the organisation take on public relations responsibility then public relations has to be there to act as a strategic adviser. The objectivity of the consultant is also a crucial skill for the in-house practitioner to acquire. Chapter 14 looks at the consultancy role, draws out the benefits of assuming such a role, but does not underestimate some of the challenges it offers.

10　The planner

Introduction

While this book is about strategic public relations leadership, it is important to cover a number of the major foundation stones of success. Planning is one such foundation stone. Excellence in planning, managing and evaluating public relations is important for two main reasons. First, it demonstrates competence in role. Chapter 12 on the technician role goes into some detail on how demonstrating technical competence provides professionals with the platform from which to take on more strategic roles. Senior managers have confidence in those who show technical proficiency. An accountant who cannot prepare a set of accounts thoroughly and professionally has no credibility. Second, using established business techniques such as recognised planning protocols also positions senior practitioners as mainstream business professionals, familiar with business processes, and a lack of general business knowledge and skills has proved to be a barrier to seniority in organisations for many public relations professionals.

This chapter will not go into the detail of planning public relations and communication campaigns since there are several excellent books on this.[1] What it will cover is:

- The context of planning
- Levels of planning
- Useful planning templates
- Key areas of focus in planning

The purpose of the chapter is to position planning as a strategic lever for the public relations leader. It is not just a process, but a mindset that provides a business stance from which to operate.

The context of planning

The context of planning has to be seen from two perspectives. The macro perspective embraces the 'big-picture' issues that were referred to in Chapter 6 (contextual intelligence). This forms the perpetual but ever-changing backdrop to all organisational activity and is the stuff that frames the interface with stakeholders. It is how the organisation influences, reacts to and deals with these issues and possible futures which determines not only its long-term prospects, but the nature and reputation of the brand in the present. Reactive organisations are always slightly behind the curve, have to respond to the lead of others and have a current reputation that reflects that. Proactive organisations are future-orientated, see opportunities as well as threats in the future and have opportunities to lead, not only because they see possible futures, but because they help to shape them. The systems and processes they put in place to monitor issues and evolving situations is part of their communicative competence, since it is only through this analysis that they can gain intelligence. This will be explored in more detail later in this chapter.

The micro perspective recognises that organisations will manage and undertake their public relations in different ways depending on the specific industry context and the way in which they are structured, operate and interact with their stakeholders. A single issue pressure group or a niche manufacturer will have a focused purpose and its stakeholders can be very specific. A large organisation such as a government department or global company will be multifaceted and have to account to a range of stakeholders who have many and different reasons for engaging with it.

As this book has already shown, understanding and analysing organisational context is critically important since public relations is both buffer and a bridge[2] to the external world and it is through communication in its broadest interpretation that stakeholders make sense of it.

The contribution of planning at various levels in the organisation

Chapter 5 explained the contribution that strategic public relations can make at the four levels at which it operates. This section will look at these four levels again, this time examining the specific contributions that a planning perspective can make. Keywords in the planning vocabulary are italicised to reinforce the points being made.

> *Societal level*: at this level public relations is focused on identifying the place of the organisation in the world and obtaining and maintaining legitimacy. In the orienter, boundary-spanning[3] role the public relations leader employs strategic planning to *monitor* and *analyse* the environment and bring *critical intelligence* to the decision-making processes within the organisation. They also *plan public relations campaigns* which are aimed at building the organisation's positioning, brand and reputation. Thus planning includes information and *intelligence inbound* and *strategic communication outbound*. However planning also has a within-system role. Its job is to constantly *review* the purpose, values and mission of the organisation, to *evaluate* the

organisation's reputational capital with a broad range of stakeholders and to inform the organisation's *strategy development* as it negotiates its contract with society.

Corporate level: at this level public relations focuses on balanced *decision-making* based on the availability of all relevant *data* pertaining to all organisational *resources* and *assets*. This includes reputational and relationship assets and the level of alignment between internal aspirations and the external expectations and experiences of a variety of legitimate stakeholders. This requires *research and analysis, insight, stakeholder engagement programmes* and constant *monitoring*. The need to *understand* the implications of corporate decisions for stakeholders and *appraise* senior managers of these is also essential at this level. In the navigator role the strategic communication leader is constantly seeking information and intelligence in order to guide the organisation as it seeks to meet its objectives.

Value-chain level: at this level communication focuses on those stakeholders who have immediate and ongoing contact with the organisation. Here, particular expertise in *stakeholder identification, segmentation, insight, engagement* and collaboration is required along with consummate skill in balancing sometimes conflicting stakeholder requirements and expectations. In this catalyst role the planner is the guardian of the value chain, *analysing, monitoring* and *evaluating* the quality of the relationships that are being developed and ensuring that the right actions are taken to gain the support of those on whom it depends (bridging). The planner is also sensitive to the fact that they will have to play a defensive role when the organisation is under attack (buffering).

Functional level: at this level the public relations leader liaises with other functional areas (such as marketing, HR and the legal department) in the organisation in order to determine the role of public relations in helping them meet organisational and departmental *objectives*. Public relations programmes will then be professionally *planned and managed* dependent on the requirements of the stakeholder groups involved. Recognised *business planning* templates, processes and systems will be used and built in order to deliver these objectives. Each plan will be different dependent on its purpose, but will be based on *evidence* and *analysis*, an underpinning *strategy*, appropriate *tactics* and will be *monitored* and *evaluated* to assess its level of success. Finally, *planning, implementing and evaluating programmes* that support overall corporate objectives is the functional responsibility of strategic communication leaders.

Having looked at the various levels at which communication has a strategic input, it can be seen that there are parallel processes operating. The first is at the macro level where the senior practitioner needs to be constantly aware of influences on the organisation which are beyond its control. The second is concerned with the micro or 'task' environment which consists of those factors, organisations, groups and individuals that the organisation interacts with regularly and which can immediately affect its performance. The task environment is normally segmented into groups of influential stakeholders with identifiable characteristics such as suppliers, customers, collaborators, regulators, competitors and activist groups. A useful segmentation of stakeholders is that provided by Bob de Wit and Ron Meyer,[4] who identify the complex web of those who would need to be taken into account at the corporate, value chain and functional levels (see Figure 10.1).

Upstream vertical (supplier) relations include providers of materials and business services, but also includes labour and information that is outside the organisation and upon which it draws. Downstream vertical (buyer) relations can be clients, customers or intermediaries who buy, sell or promote the products and services of the organisation. Direct horizontal (industry insider) relations involves relationships between the organisations and others in their industry – their peer organisations. Indirect (industry outsider) relations are where an organisation has relationships with those outside its industry, for example those who provide complementary services or products such as a chain of hotels working with a carpet manufacturer. Sociocultural actors are those organisations that have an influence on societal values, beliefs and behaviours such as the media, community groups and non-governmental organisations (NGOs).

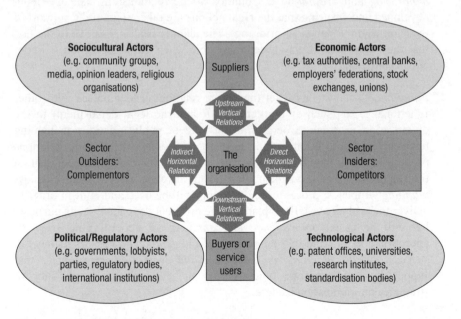

Figure 10.1 De Wit and Meyer's web of relational actors

Source: Adapted from R. de Wit and R. Meyer (2010). *Strategy: Process, Content, Context*. London: Thomson, p. 36.

Economic actors include central banks, stock exchanges, taxation authorities and trade organisations. Political/legal actors include, for example, government, regulatory bodies, international institutions and international NGOs such as the International Court of Human Rights. Technological actors influence the pace and direction of technological developments and create new knowledge, for instance universities, research bodies, government agencies and inventors.

This analysis makes the point that organisations are held in a network of stakeholder relationships who ultimately gave the organisation 'permission' to exist by supporting its 'licence to operate'.

It might be thought that this parallel process of analysing the macro and micro environments is more to do with identifying strategic business issues rather than public relations. This is precisely the point. These issues will force some sort of action from the organisation and action always has public relations dimensions. Indeed, the most impactful strategic public relations programmes address the issues that organisations face.

Strategic planning models and templates

John Thompson and Frank Martin say that strategy is 'the means by which organisations achieve (and seek to achieve) their objectives and purposes'.[5] Strategic management is the 'process by which an organisation establishes its objectives, formulates actions (strategies) designed to meet these objectives in the desired timescale, implements the actions, and assesses progress and results'. Strategic communication planning models and templates closely align with this process. Research among Europe's public relations community[6] indicates that 91 per cent of them plan and execute public relations programmes that directly contribute to these goals.

The planning models that are outlined in this chapter are based on what is called the systems view of organisations. We believe the 'open system' is an important concept because it proposes that an organisation is a 'living entity with boundaries, inputs, outputs, "throughputs", and enough feedback from both the internal and external environments so that it can make appropriate adjustments in time to keep on living'.[7] In other words, open systems are responsive, dynamic organisms which receive, process and initiate information and activity and are in a state of constant flux, set within a context which itself is in flux. That to us reflects organisational life today.

All strategic planning models follow a basic four-step sequence. Step one concerns a thorough understanding of the current situation; step two is about setting aims and choosing the appropriate strategy to achieve those aims; step three involves implementing the strategy; and step four consists of monitoring progress for corrective action or evaluating the final outcomes. It was back in 1979 that John Marston developed the public relations planning acronym RACE (Research, Action, Communication and Evaluation),[8] with the American academics Scott Cutlip, Alan Center and Glenn Broom developing what the authors believe to be one of the most helpful public relations models which is provided in Figure 10.2.[9] The planning model devised by one of us[10] shown in Figure 10.3 captures the essence of the best-known planning approaches[11] in an extended sequence of steps.

While it is recognised that most strategic communication leaders will be perfectly familiar with planning models which follow the basic pattern of those shown, it is the experience of the authors that there are some elements of the planning process that are more problematic than others and it is to these areas that this chapter now turns it attention.

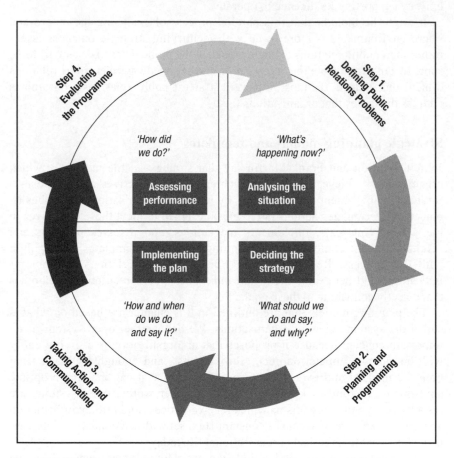

Figure 10.2 Cutlip, Center and Broom's public relations planning model

Source: Adapted from S.M. Cutlip, A.H. Center and G.M. Broom (2010). *Effective Public Relations* (10th edn). Upper Saddle River, NJ: Pearson Prentice Hall, p. 283

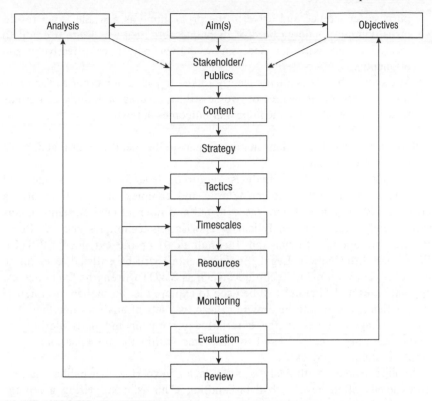

Figure 10.3 Gregory's planning model

Source: A. Gregory (2010). *Planning and Managing Public Relations Campaigns* (3rd edn). London: Kogan Page, p. 42

Problem areas in planning

The strategic planning models above have a logic and flow to them which suggests that each element is linked to and flows from the previous one. However, a general observation is that there are a number of core issues with many plans. In brief these are:

- Plans often appear to be written in siloed sections. Deep and professional analysis does not always appear to be clearly linked to the courses of action that are being recommended and the tactics that are suggested.
- Plans have unrealistic objectives; they over-promise and underestimate the complexity of the task in hand, particularly when this relates to behaviour change.
- Plans regularly lack a strategy: they move from objectives or more often from messages to tactics without a bridging rationale which provides

purpose, coherence and drive to the programme as a whole. As a result, plans contain a smorgasbord of disparate activities which are a credit to creativity, but will not necessarily deliver objectives effectively and efficiently.

* The stated objectives are not clearly linked to evaluation criteria. Too often there are 'proxy' measures or, worse still, measures of activity or outputs which are not related to the impact or outcomes of the plan.

With these general observations in mind, what are the specific areas that deserve more detailed comment?

Analysis. The level of analysis required depends on the scope and complexity of the plan. The most large and complex plans will involve a thorough investigation of both the external and internal environments as has been already indicated. Analytical categorisation techniques such as PEST (Political, Economic, Social and Technological) or the extended EPISTLE (PEST plus Information, Legal, Environmental) will be enlisted to examine the external environment. Techniques such as SWOT (Strengths, Weaknesses, Opportunities and Threats) will be used to explore the internal environment.[12] The challenge appears to be drawing these two sets of analyses together. The key is linkages. Issues in the external environment and particularly with stakeholders are usually linked to problems within the organisation; either people, systems or processes.

Another problem with analysis is the lack of expertise that public relations professionals often have with data-handling. This is unsurprising given the background that many professionals come from. Recognising this deficiency is important and need not be a cause for embarrassment – that is what trained business analysts and consultants are for. Collecting data is one thing, but analysing it and drawing the correct conclusions from it is quite another and it is critically important that the evidence-base on which strategic communication plans are founded is valid and properly interpreted. It is worth considering paying for professional interpretation of the data rather than for its collection if choices have to be made.

Aims and objectives. Agreeing realistic aims and objectives is complicated. Thorough analysis will have revealed the scope, size and nature of the public relations task and therefore the time, resources and expertise required to tackle it. Aims state what the plan seeks to achieve in overall terms, and should be agreed as appropriate with senior managers and linked to organisational aims. A good aim is able to be evaluated at the end of the planning period by being turned into a question. Hence, if the aim is to build relationships with new suppliers in an emerging market then it can be evaluated by asking the question, 'Were relationships built with new suppliers in this market?'

Objectives are the specific and measurable steps that break the aims into what could be regarded as the milestones for the plan. There is a hierarchy of three levels of objectives:[13]

* *Awareness objectives* concern information and knowledge. They focus on providing the *cognitive*, or thinking, element of programme content and on what information stakeholders should know, understand and remember.
* *Acceptance objectives* are concerned with how stakeholders react to information. This is what the *affective*, or emotional, reactions the content is meant to evoke. This relates to interests and attitudes.
* *Action objectives* relate to the hoped for behavioural response. This focuses on the *connotative*, or action, outcomes that are generated when stakeholders are exposed to the content of the programme.

Clearly, it is usually more difficult to achieve behavioural objectives than thinking objectives, the notable exception being hot issues. So, the level of effect (or outcome) anticipated from the objectives set should be chosen with care.

Apart from lack of clarity over the different levels of objectives and the related evaluations, there is often a mixing of *outcome* and *process* aims and objectives. Outcome aims and objectives relate to what the planner wants *stakeholders to do*, the results or impact of the programme. Process aims are framed around what *the planner does* to achieve the aim. Thus, 'maximise the number of employees enrolling in the staff volunteering scheme' is an outcome aim. The aim could have been stated as 'use all available company web-based communication channels to maximise the number of employees enrolling in the staff volunteering scheme'. This includes process as well as an outcome. The authors regularly see objectives such as 'maximise use of social media' or 'deliver a cost-effective programme' without any acknowledgement that these sorts of objectives are very different from outcome objectives, and indeed they are often there to demonstrate activity levels, not value-added.

Stakeholders/publics. Just two comments to make on this topic. First, it is becoming increasingly difficult to identify stakeholders and particularly publics. While De Wit and Meyer's web of relational actors mentioned earlier is useful, it is not exhaustive. As one of the CEO's mentioned to one of us, 'These days I have no idea who will contact me, where they live or anything about them'. Some stakeholders are relatively easy to group and define, for example local politicians, but it is becoming increasingly difficult in a global and interconnected world to identify stakeholders or to categorise them according to the nature of their stake. Indeed, there are some authors[14] who contend that it is becoming impossible to categorise stakeholders in any meaningful way, particularly in the online world, not only because it is difficult to detect the nature of their stake, but because of their fluidity. Stakeholders move in and out of a stakeholding relationship with frequency, for unpredictable lengths of time and for unpredictable reasons.

Second it is helpful to point out the difference between a stakeholder and publics although these words are often used interchangeably. According to public relations academics James Grunig and Fred Repper[15] stakeholders describe categories of people who are affected by the decisions of an organisation or who can themselves affect the organisation; thus, employees and investors are stakeholders. Many stakeholders remain passive, but when they become aware and active they become 'publics'. Publics form when the behaviour of an organisation causes consequences for them and they organise to do something in response. Hence, publics can cut across stakeholder groupings, for example if an organisation causes local pollution, community groups, local government, government environment agencies as well as employees could become active. The point is that publics collect around issues and whatever descriptor is used, this is a useful way to categorise those groups with whom the organisation interacts. A careful analysis of the *issues* that an organisation may cause or that may impact upon it will reveal those groups who are likely to be active.

   Content. Most traditional planning models use the word messages rather than content and it is true to say that message design and distribution to achieve awareness and to persuade has been a feature of public relations practice. Indeed, there are many kinds of campaigns where messages are essential, particularly in public information campaigns. Road safety messages are encapsulated in slogans such as 'tiredness kills'. However, messages are clearly one-way and to evaluate them the originator simply checks to see if they have been received and acted on. Messaging is inappropriate if an organisation genuinely wants to enter a dialogue where the outcome will be mutually determined. Irrespective of the developments in social media and mobile technologies that force organisations into dialogue, collaboration and cooperation are in the long run and with most stakeholders the most effective way to build lasting relationships. Of course Return On Engagement (ROE) is much more complex to measure than receipt of messages and rather more sophisticated evaluation techniques which measure the quality of relationships[16] will be required.

   Strategy. Many public relations plans move directly from objectives or content to tactics without having any cohesive and coherent strategy. Strategy is the most difficult part of the planning process and there is remarkable confusion about what it actually is. Strategy forms the backbone of the programme holding all the parts together. The preceding analysis about the context of the programme, issues, objectives, stakeholders and content leads to the point where the platform for tactical activity is determined: it is the fulcrum. Strategy is the rationale that moves the planner from where they are now to where they want to be. It is sometimes called 'the big idea', or an all embracing concept, but it need not be. What is important is that the programme of action has a clear rationale against which tactical ideas can be benchmarked as being acceptable or not. In a nutshell, strategy is *how* the objective will be achieved and tactics are *what* is to be done.

   Evaluation. There are numerous books and publications that go into detail on how to evaluate strategic public relations programmes,[17] so this will not be examined in great detail here. However, there are two major problems that persist in evaluation. The first is a search for the 'silver bullet': that single evaluation measure that will demonstrate Return On Investment (ROI). There is no silver bullet and to look for it betrays a lack of appreciation of the complexity of human relationships. What strategic programmes do have is clear, realistic and measurable objectives of the kind indicated above and planners must therefore demonstrate their performance against them and also be aware of the unintended effects (for good and ill) that some programmes have.

The second issue relates to what is called 'level substitution'. Evaluation normally takes place at five levels: *input*, which is what the planner puts in to their public relations products, for example content and design; *output*, which is how effectively products are distributed and used by target groups, for example how many employees received the e-newsletter; *outtake*, is what the target group extracted from the communication, for example the newsletter content employees remember; *outcome*, which is the impact of the communication, for example how many employees took up the offer of free well-being checks; and *outflow*, which is the long-term reputational impact of the programme. Level substitution involves setting an objective at one level and then measuring it at another, usually lower, level. For example, the objective might be to make a particular stakeholder group aware of impending legislation. The only real way to measure this is to ask them, then their awareness can be properly assessed; this is an outcome measure. However, often evaluations are done at the level of output; for example planners will claim that awareness has been raised because they are able to give statistical evidence of the number of unique visitors to a website providing the information about the legislation. Level substitution continues to be a problem that bedevils the public relations industry, particularly in the area of media measurement where the outputs – clippings or hits are counted – and outcomes are not measured.

Summary

This chapter has stressed the importance of planning as a fundamental building block in public relations leadership. Competence in planning is a key indicator of competence in role. The chapter has stressed the importance of the context in which planning takes place, both in terms of the macro issues and the micro or task issues that dictate what the nature of planned programmes will be. It has also identified that planning has a role to play at all levels in the organisation. The selection of models and templates is typical of those that are widely used, but despite knowledge of these, the issues that have been raised as problem areas are persistent. Mastery of programme planning is a fundamental essential in the kit bag of the strategic public relations leader and a principal lever of credibility.

Notes

1 There are a number of books which focus on planning, or which have good sections on planning within them, such as: Broom, G.M. (2009). *Cutlip and Center's Effective Public Relations*, 8th edition. Upper Saddle River, NJ: Prentice Hall; Gregory, A. (2010). *Planning and Managing Public Relations Campaigns*, 3rd edition. London: Kogan Page; Harrison, K. (2011). *Strategic Public Relations: A Practical Guide to Success*. South Yarra: Palgrave Macmillan; Moss, D. and DeSanto, B. (2011). *Public Relations: A Managerial Perspective*. Los Angeles, CA: Sage; Smith, R.D. (2009).

Strategic Planning for Public Relations, 3rd edition. Mahwah, NJ: Lawrence Erlbaum Associates.

2 Meznar, M.B. and Nigh, D. (1995). Buffer or bridge: environmental determinants of public affairs activities in American firms, *Academy of Management Journal*, 38(4), 975–96.

3 White, J. and Dozier, D.M. (1992). Public relations and management decision making. In Grunig, J.E. (ed.), *Excellence in Public Relations and Communication Management*. Hillsdown, NJ: Lawrence Erlbaum Associates.

4 De Wit, R. and Meyer, R. (2010). *Strategy: Process, Content, Context*. London: Thomson, p. 361.

5 Thompson, J. and Martin, F. (2010) *Strategic Management: Awareness and Change*. Andover: Cengage Learning EMEA, p. 790.

6 Zerfass, A., Verhoeven, P., Tench, R., Moreno, A., and Verčič, D. (2011). *European Communication Monitor 2011: Empirical Insights into Strategic Communication in Europe*. Results of an Empirical Survey in 43 Countries (Chart Version). Brussels: EACD, EUPRERA (available at: www.communicationmonitor.eu).

7 McElreath, M.P. (1997). *Managing Systematic and Ethical Public Relations Campaigns*, 2nd edition. Madison, WI: Brown and Benchmark.

8 Marston, J.E. (1979). *Modern Public Relations*. New York: McGraw-Hill.

9 Broom, G.M. (2009). *Cutlip and Center's Effective Public Relations* (see above).

10 Gregory, A. (2010). *Planning and Managing Public Relations Campaigns* (see above).

11 For example, those provided by Broom, G.M. (2009). *Cutlip and Center's Effective Public Relations* (see above); Harrison, K. (2011). *Strategic Public Relations* (see above); Moss, D. and DeSanto, B. (2011). *Public Relations* (see above); Smith, R.D. (2009). *Strategic Planning for Public Relations* (see above).

12 Gregory, A. (2010). *Planning and Managing Public Relations Campaigns* (see above).

13 Smith, R.D. (2009). *Strategic Planning for Public Relations* (see above).

14 Pal, M. and Dutta, M. J. (2008) Public relations in a global context: the relevance of critical modernism as a theoretical lens, *Journal of Public Relations Research*, 20(2), 159–79.

15 Grunig, J.E. and F.C. Repper (1992). Strategic management, publics and issues. In Grunig, J.E. (ed.). *Excellence in Public Relations and Communication Management*. Hillsdale, NJ: Lawrence Erlbaum Associates.

16 Hon, L.C. and Grunig, J.E. (1999) *Guidelines for Measuring Relationships in Public Relations*. Gainesville, FL: Institute for Public Relations. Available at www.instituteforpr.org/wp-content/uploads/Guidelines_Measuring_Relationships.pdf.

17 For example, the COI guide to Return on Marketing Investment can be found at http://coi.gov.uk/blogs/bigthinkers/wp-content/uploads/2009/11/coi-payback-and-romi-paper.pdf. See also Van Ruler, B., Tkalac Verčič, A. and Verčič, D. (2008) *Public Relations Metrics: Research and Evaluation*. New York: Routledge; and Watson, T. and Noble, P. (2010) *Evaluating Public Relations*, 2nd edition. London: Kogan Page.

11 The catalyst

Introduction

When Kevin Murray and Jon White interviewed chief executives about working with high-calibre public relations advisers they found:

> This breed of person showed an acute understanding of stakeholder needs and desires, and awareness of the organisation's business model and key performance indicators, and awareness of the operating environment and the confidence to challenge the leaders of the organisation ('to look them in the eye').[1]

The model outlined in Chapter 5 concludes by suggesting four roles for public relations leaders: orienter, navigator, catalyst and implementer. In this chapter we will focus on the catalyst role. This requires special attention because it is so critically important and because it has rarely been focused on. The other roles are embedded across the whole of the book, but with a significant part of the implementer role also being covered in Chapter 12 – the expert technician.

As implied, the organisational catalyst is someone who makes things happen, but in a very particular way. Leaders make things happen in their areas of responsibility. As the organisational catalyst, public relations leaders also make things happen to support and defend the values and relationships which are all so critical to organisational success as a whole. They examine the touch points between an organisation and its stakeholders, not only for those stakeholding groups for whom they hold professional responsibility. This may mean operating in other leaders' territory, and pointing out where systems and processes do not deliver against values and expectations. The catalyst acts as the organisation's general guardian and fixer. This role as 'fixer' is a potential source of power for practitioners and can be leveraged to reinforce personal leadership authority beyond technical competence (more on this later).

As indicated in Chapter 5, the catalyst role comes into play largely at the value-chain level, with those close stakeholders who interact with the organisation on a regular basis. However, as will be pointed out later, the catalyst operates at all levels in the organisation. In this chapter, we will explore the organisational catalyst under four headings:

- The need for a catalyst
- Implications
- Grit in the oyster
- Areas of influence

The need for a catalyst

In recent times there has been an increasing recognition that organisations are operating under a new business paradigm. As South African Benita Steyn says, business organisations have been focused on the bottom line.[2] Return on investment and profit have been the mantra. Now, 'social, political, environmental, and ethical issues have gained strategic importance, all strategic stakeholders as well as societal values and norms have to be considered'. Trust and legitimacy are not 'nice to have'; they are essential. Ultimately, society decides whether it will give an organisation a licence to operate.[3] The opprobrium that banks are currently experiencing reflects the view that people in general believe they have acted illegitimately. The anger felt is partly the result of the fact that they have proved too large and important to have their licence withdrawn. Many, but not all chief executives realise the far-reaching nature and implications of these new accountabilities and are trying to deal with a world full of new risks that are not amenable to traditional solutions such as more efficient working practices, increased resources or tighter compliance. They need an organisational catalyst who can identify the risks and issues in organisational performance from relationship and communicative perspectives and who – most crucially – offers solutions. So, for example, if cumbersome compliance systems are preventing productive relationships with suppliers, this needs to be identified and fixed by someone who looks across the whole organisation and whose responsibility it is to identify potential issues and threats to the organisation's reputation. As Steyn says, 'Contemporary concepts such as reputation, trust, legitimacy, transparency, governance, socially responsible behaviour, and sustainable development are monopolising strategic conversations in this century.'[4]

The public relations practitioner is well placed to lead on these issues. Their knowledge and leadership in these areas can also become an important source of power.[5] Power within organisations has been seen to elude public relations professionals because they have been traditionally reliant on their skills of persuasion, their ability to build strong interpersonal relationships, network and undertake technical tasks effectively.[6] Like it or not, coercive power is vital to gain leverage in the organisational structure. Being responsible for initiating discussions about how to fix the issues linked with organisation-critical assets such as reputation and trust puts organisational catalysts in a different and better place. They are able to determine and direct courses of action to enhance and block threats to the organisation's reputation. It has been a harsh lesson to learn in numerous organisations such as BP in Texas and Barclays Bank who have discovered that where governance and reputational risks are not handled well the threat of organisational failure is as acute as the immediate financial fallout. In light of this, the organisational catalyst calls for leaders to reflect regularly and seriously on the purpose, values, actions and words of the enterprise and whether or not they will retain support.

It is interesting that in these times of increasing uncertainty and accountability, the number of public relations professionals on boards is increasing and one of their roles is to be the guardian of strategic issues and risks.[7]

Implications

So what, then, are the implications of these requirements?

First, the organisational catalyst is both an ideological and contextual leader.[8] Ideological leadership may have negative connotations, but what we mean here is carving out a role for the organisation in its immediate value-chain network, which is unique to itself and which adds real value. This is not about *imposing* the organisation on the value chain, which is ultimately futile, but sustainable enterprises find a place where they add value and are valued, not only economically, but as partners and as peers with common aspirations. This begins to determine the nature of relationships with immediate stakeholders and in turn demonstrates to the wider 'general public' in very concrete terms how its values and character operate in action.

Contextual leadership is about managing multiple, multi-layered and interwoven relationships between the members of the value chain, and beyond that, the relationships on which they depend. For example, an organisation may supply goods and services to another organisation. That second organisation may also be supplied by others who have connections which may be problematic or beneficial. The first organisation will need to take a view on these relationships and the organisational catalyst will be the one to both obtain information through intelligence gathering and make an assessment of required actions. These will be for the benefit not only of the first organisation, but for the whole value chain, since potentially the whole chain will be affected. So, if it is discovered that one member of the value chain has particularly strong and credible connections with local communities, that is an asset that the whole value chain may benefit from.

Ideological and contextual leadership is a strategic process, it is not about *doing* public relations, but at the heart of determining what an organisation's purposes, place and role is in the value chain.

The second implication is that the catalyst views the organisation from the standpoint of those others in the value chain. Their principal test will be to ask whether the organisation delivers on the promises it makes, and this goes beyond compliance. As the most recent Edelman Trust Barometer[9] concludes, to move from licence to operate to a licence to lead requires 'principles-based leadership not rules-based performance'. A further test will be how selfish the organisation is perceived to be. Does it operate in a spirit of partnership and mutuality seeking to ensure the well-being of the whole value chain, or is it constantly seeking its own advantage?

The task of the organisational catalyst is to walk in the shoes of its value-chain partners to see the organisation as it is in reality: its actual behaviours and actions. Undertaking an audit of the organisation from a value-chain perspective is a revealing exercise. Figure 11.1 uses added value and trust as axes in this exercise.

The third implication of being an organisational catalyst requires the public relations professional to be a reflective leader. Reflection is not a passive kind of leadership and not to be confused with reflexivity. Reflexive leaders, according to Susanne Holmstrom,[10] take an internal perspective; they tend therefore to repeat established behaviours and actions, and are blind to the shifting and broader context. This exposes them to risk because actions and decisions can be seen to be out of kilter with what is happening 'out there'. They will therefore find their world-view in conflict with other world-views. We find this quite often with companies who are led by strong entrepreneurs with single-minded purpose or by scientists and engineers who take a very rational approach to their work. In the case of entrepreneurs this can be a good thing, leading to innovations of mind-blowing scale, but it can also lead to catastrophic failure when they are seen to be out of touch with what the public wants. Famously, Shell, in its

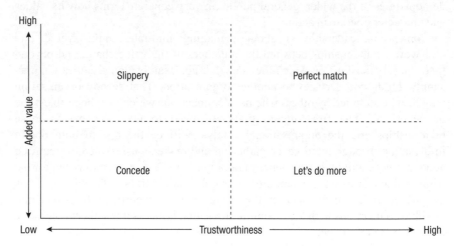

Figure 11.1 Value-chain auditing

Note:

Map each value-chain member onto the grid by asking two questions:

- If I were organisation X in my value chain, how would I rate my organisation in terms of adding value?
- How would I rate our organisation as being trustworthy?

It would be even better if you asked independent researchers to do this.

disposal of the Brent Spar oil platform, took all the right engineering decisions, but was blind to the consequences of not taking into account the fact that environmental activism was rising on the agenda and that Greenpeace was able to provoke an emotional response.

Reflective leaders, on the other hand, see their organisations as part of a multi-dimensional and multi-contextual world, and there are a number of aspects to this that play to the strengths of public relations leaders:

- the organisation sees itself from outside, as one actor among many and set within a larger context;
- the organisation has choices and the potential to act and behave differently;
- others realise this too and hold it accountable for those choices;
- this frames the relationships that the organisation forms with stakeholders;
- this is a critical factor when assessing risks and opportunities.

The person (or department) who takes responsibility for generating intelligence on these factors is of major significance to the organisation. It is an obvious role for public relations.

This perspective leads to a new approach to the positioning of the organisation, which can be seen to be complementary or even an alternative to traditional strategic and marketing thinking. Rather than just looking for competitive advantage (Porter) or to lever resources (the resource-based view), the organisation seeks to find a place in the value chain where it can add value. So instead of stakeholders having to be 'managed', they are respected: instead of depending on 'getting our message across' the organisation becomes part of an ongoing and multiple polylogue where listening takes on a critical importance: where the primary role of public relations is not information dissemination, but intelligence acquisition. In this way the public relations leader becomes, in Benita Steyn's words, 'the reflective strategist',[11] the outcome of which, for that individual, is to become the source of constant challenge, change and renewal; the catalyst in the organisation, the grit in the oyster whose constant but constructive irritation produces something of immense value.

Grit in the oyster

From the above it can be seen that the catalyst role, although focused on the way things are done in the value chain, operates at all the levels mentioned in Chapter 5. At the societal level, the knowledge of context and social change needs to be factored into the developing strategy of the organisation. At the corporate level decisions need to be illuminated with stakeholder and contextual intelligence and constantly measured against purpose and values. At the functional level too, public relations and broader communication-led programmes, whether internal or external, need framing within this context. It has always been a puzzle to us that a constant challenge cited by public relations professionals is aligning public relations and business strategy.[12] How can this be if the catalyst public relations leader is doing their job properly?

This last point might be partly explained by the observation that being the organisational catalyst is not a comfortable role. It takes personal courage, credibility, a great deal of persistence, resilience and integrity – along with evidence. However, research by one of us[13] has demonstrated that such public relations leaders are not afraid to elevate uncomfortable truths to the board and indeed that is why they are valued.[14] Unfortunately, the skills, knowledge and behaviours required to fulfil this role are rarely taught either on advanced public relations courses or management programmes. Perhaps the nearest equivalent to this role is that of the management consultant and we cover the internal consultant role in Chapter 14.

It also has to be recognised that dealing in organisational relationships (internal and external) cannot be dissociated from organisational politics and power. As mentioned earlier, because of the risk involved in working in this territory and their ability to deal with it, public relations leaders can attain coercive power with the ability to direct action. The received wisdom on this is that the practitioner therefore should be on the board. However, there is counter-thinking on this which is worth exploring. Derina Holtzhausen and colleagues take the view that public relations leaders should 'resist authoritative organisational power structures' even when they hold senior positions because they should assume the role of organisational activist.[15] Indeed, she argues that being in the senior decision-making cadre may severely restrict the public relations leader from this activist role. Championing those who do not have power, whether they be within or outside the organisation, and constantly challenging the status quo, bringing in alternative perspectives and voices, actually makes the organisation stronger. In fact, this activist role can be taken one step further to become the character of the whole organisation. She cites the case of the Benetton group who have taken on the corporate activist role on issues such as AIDS, the death penalty and racial prejudice – often to the outrage of the 'establishment'.

While this may seem an extreme and even self-serving position, there are merits in this view. As one director of corporate affairs told us, 'If I have not had a row with my MD by 9.00 in the morning, I'm not doing my job properly.' It is the job of catalysts to constantly challenge. The Swedish academic and practitioner Sven Hamrefors captures the role amusingly but well when he compares the catalyst leader to the medieval court jester whose role it was to tell the king how things really were because the king, like many chief executives, was usually told what he wanted to hear by his courtiers.[16] The jester had a formal and protected position to ensure that grounded reality was also given a voice and for the king to see himself as others saw him. As the quote from Kevin Murray and Jon White at the beginning of this chapter affirms, the catalyst needs the confidence to look the chief executive in the eye.

Areas of influence

As mentioned above, the organisational catalyst has a part to play at all levels of the organisation. They are also uniquely placed to look at the *whole* organisation, in context, as others see it and very specifically from the point of view of those in the value chain – including employees. Public relations practitioners are some of the few people to have this helicopter view of the organisation, seeing the whole system within a wider system. This cross-cutting role is important. We all know situations where various parts of an organisation have a role in an activity and issues are caused by those actions in aggregate. The organisational catalyst will appreciate from a relationship point of view that this is corrosive and seek to fix it by encouraging departments to work together to resolve any problems.

Beyond these vertical and horizontal responsibilities there are a number of other areas that the catalyst will need to monitor and be involved in:

Change leadership and management. It is agreed that public relations is usually involved in change-management programmes. Leadership is also associated strongly with change (see Chapter 3). However, it is not the *content* and *outcomes* of these programmes that is the point here, but the impact of their implementation on the system. The reality is that most change-management programmes are not followed through, or the next one arises before the first one is completed. The effect of this is system cynicism,[17] and inertia and resistance to further change because 'we've seen it all before and if we keep our heads down long enough, we'll get back to where we are now'. The role of the catalyst is therefore to make judgements about the timeliness of such programmes, their nature and audit their progress and impact. In a world where constant adaption and change are required, inertia and those things causing inertia are the enemies of progress.

The catalyst's knowledge is invaluable when considering organisational structures. Key questions need to be asked about what should be retained centrally and what can be localised. The principle of subsidiarity, that is allowing decision-making, especially about implementation, to be done at the point where those decisions bite, is an important one. Equally important is listening to feedback on how structures can be adjusted to make them better.

Organisational structure tells a story as does the physical structure of buildings and the location of people within them. The hierarchical structure of an organisation can often be replicated in the physical layout of buildings: senior managers on the top floor, reserved parking, dingy restrooms for cleaning staff. They all speak volumes about the organisation.

Apart from managerial hierarchies and physical structures, organisational structures are also mentally constructed. The way that vision and values are discussed and agreed set the frame. Organisational language, forms of address and the way people are around each other creates not only the culture of the organisation, but the uncoded approvals and disapprovals that configure the mind-set of employees. The organisational catalyst remains in tune with these things, looking for issues and initiating actions which build the whole system positively.

While structures set the architecture, processes are the organisational software. They move things around the system: in, out, through, around and between. It is often process or a combination of structure and process that causes friction. 'Why is it so difficult to get things done?' is a voiced frustration against dysfunctional structure and process. A simple audit of all the steps required to achieve a particular end will reveal the blockages, bottlenecks and redundancies that are inherent in any process that is built up over periods of time. Custom and practice become the norm. The ambition of the catalyst has to be, as Sven Hamrefors says,[18] to have systems that are better than actually needed. He also points out that benchmarking against those in the same industry sector rarely brings significant improvements and gives the example of a budget airline learning from supermarket logistics about how to turn around baggage quickly as cross-sector thinking.

The catalyst examines processes to discover the real issues that produce conflict in relationships and which pose reputational threats. He or she then comes up with solutions, usually working with those with the knowledge, invariably those who are involved at the front-line.

The ultimate objective for the catalyst is for the organisation to function to its optimum capability within a value chain and wider stakeholding community. These are the constituencies that will judge everything that is done, said and demonstrated through decision-making, structure, systems and processes.

Summary

This chapter has sought to demonstrate the role of the organisational catalyst. As one of our vice-chancellors said to us, 'How is it that wherever there is action your PR students are in the middle of it?' That is exactly it. The catalyst is where the action is, present throughout the organisation at all levels; observing structures, systems, processes and indeed every activity where the reality needs fixing.

The communicating organisation is not a choice. Organisations communicate whether they want to or not. The organisational catalyst's job is to look at the organisation in its totality, to see where the potential friction points are and to ensure that action is taken to fix them. Why is this the role of the public relations leader? Because there is no one better placed to do this. Public relations leaders are invited onto boards not because they can create wonderful communication plans, but because their perspectives and insights contribute to the future well-being of the organisation. Being the catalyst, ensuring the organisation is communicatively competent and defending the intangible asset base is the job for a leader, the public relations leader.

Notes

1 Murray, K. and White, J. (2005). CEO's views on reputation management, *Journal of Communication Management*, 9(4), 348–58, p. 354.
2 Steyn, B. (2009). The strategic role of public relations is strategic reflection: a South African research stream, *American Behavioral Scientist*, 53(4), 516–32, pp. 517–18.
3 Broom, G.M. and Dozier, D.M. (1990) *Using Research in Public Relations: Applications to Programme Management*, Englewood Cliffs, NJ: Prentice Hall.
4 Steyn, B. (2009). The strategic role of public relations is strategic reflection, p. 517 (see above).
5 One of the classic texts on power and still widely used today is by French, J. and Raven, B. (1959). The Bases of Social Power. In Ott, J. Parkes, S. and Simpson, R. (eds), *Classic Readings in Organizational Behavior* (pp. 400–9). Belmont, CA: Wadsworth. They describe five sources of power: coercive, where punishment can be inflicted if expected behaviour is not complied with; reward, where someone has power to incentivise another, for example giving a discretionary bonus; legitimate, where someone is obliged to submit to another, for example a subordinate to their senior manager; referent, where there is close identification between one and another, for example where there is a strong team ethos, and expert, where one has superior knowledge. Raven also argued for another power – informational, where someone has superior persuasive and communication powers to influence others.
6 For more evidence on this see Zerfass, A., Verhoeven, P., Tench, R., Moreno, A. and Verčič, D. (2011). *European Communication Monitor 2011: Empirical Insights into Strategic Communication in Europe. Results of an Empirical Survey in 43 Countries (Chart Version)*. Brussels: EACD, EUPRERA; and Hogg, G. and Doolan, D. (1999). Playing the part: practitioner roles in public relations, *European Journal of Marketing*, 33(5/6), 597–611.
7 The European Communications Monitor (Zerfass, A., Verčič, D., Verhoeven, P., Moreno, A. and Tench, R. (2012). *European Communication Monitor 2012: Challenges and Competencies for Strategic Communication. Results of an Empirical Survey in 42 Countries*. Brussels: EACD/EUPRERA) and the American Generally Accepted Practices (GAPVII) Study published by the USC Annenberg Strategic Communication and Public Relations Center (available at http://ascjwcb.org/gapstudy) provide the latest insights on this.
8 The ideological and contextual leader concepts come from research done for the Swedish Institute of Public Relations by Professor Sven Hamrefors (2010) which is provided in a report called *The Information Officer's Role in Leadership*, Stockholm: The Swedish Institute of Public Relations.
9 Edelman Trust Barometer (2012). London: Edelman. Available at http://edelmaneditions.com/wp-content/uploads/2012/01/Final-Brochure-1.16.pdf.
10 Holmstrom, S. (2005). Co-evolution of society and organization: reflexivity, contingency and reflection. Paper given at EUPRERA Conference, Lisbon, 10–13 November.
11 Steyn, B. (2009). The strategic role of public relations is strategic reflection, pp. 517–18 (see above).
12 This is seen as the second largest challenge in the most recent European Communications Monitor, Zerfass, A., Verčič, D., Verhoeven, P., Moreno, A. and Tench, R. (2012). *European Communication Monitor 2012* (see above).
13 Gregory, A. (2008). The competencies of senior practitioners in the UK: an initial study, *Public Relations Review*, 34(3), 215–23.
14 Murray, K. and White, J. (2005). CEO's views on reputation management, p. 354 (see above).
15 Derina Holtzhausen is a leading scholar in what is called the postmodern school of public relations. Papers worth reading are Holtzhausen, D.R. (2000). Postmodern

values in public relations, *Journal of Public Relations Research*, 12(1), 93–114; Holtzhausen, D.R. and Voto, R. (2002). Resistance from the margins: the postmodern public relations practitioner as organisational activist, *Journal of Public Relations Research*, 14(1), 57–84.

16 Hamrefors, S. (2010). *The Information Officer's Role in Leadership* (see above).

17 See Qian, Y. and Daniels, T.D. (2008). A communication model of employee cynicism toward organisational change, *Corporate Communications: An International Journal*, 13(3), 319–32.

18 Hamrefors, S. (2010). *The Information Officer's Role in Leadership* (see above).

12 The expert technician

Introduction

Being an accomplished communication technician is an essential part of public relations leadership. The sort of technical skills usually associated with public relations include writing, content development, making a presentation, negotiating with others and carrying out research.[1] These are the practical abilities practitioners display in their key areas of operation such as media relations, crisis management, marketing communication and employee engagement. As with other professions such as accounting and law, demonstrating technical proficiency is necessary if public relations practitioners wish to be considered for executive management positions. Having reached such senior positions in the organisation, public relations leaders continue to display high-level technical skills in tandem with their role as a strategic adviser to the CEO and other executives. This might include high-level media briefings linked to mergers and acquisitions, crisis communication and political lobbying.

Although drawing from a similar knowledge bank, it is important from a personal development perspective to understand how the technical capabilities of a public relations leader differ from those required of a new starter to the profession or a middle manager. This chapter explores this issue. In doing so, it highlights an essential qualitative difference in the technical proficiency required of public relations leaders.

The chapter begins by highlighting three reasons why technical know-how is generally important. The chapter then discusses research that explores the idea of professional expertise and what it entails. This perspective is introduced because it highlights that technical skill is an integrated phenomenon. The most accomplished performers not only understand methods and routines but also have a heightened appreciation of how and when to use them. They exhibit situational sensitivity, flexibility and improvisational skill. The emphasis becomes about contextual intelligence and how individual leaders continually adapt and reconfigure their technical knowledge to cope with an uncertain environment (also see Chapter 6). To illustrate the point the chapter compares the skills required of a novice, intermediate and expert practitioner in a media relations context. This discussion leads to the conclusion that interpersonal communication skills are pivotal to the maintenance of technical mastery in the field of public relations leadership.

The purpose of the chapter is not to provide a 'how do' guide on key technical aspects of practice. The aim is instead to provoke a reflection on the importance of technical skills in a leadership context and what it is to be a public relations expert. The chapter is therefore divided into the following sections:

* Technician is not a dirty word
* What is an expert?
* From novice to media relations expert
* Making sense of the media environment
* Developing and maintaining expertise

Technician is not a dirty word

There is no shame in a public relations leader continuing to be recognised as a good technician. Being a leader is not all about strategy, vision and directing others. In fact, good technical skills can enhance the public relations practitioner's standing as a leader. Even competence in basic tasks, such as the ability to write a good speech or a compelling article, can enhance a leader's personal credibility within the public relations department as well as across the organisation. Writing in the *Harvard Business Review*, Rob Goffee and Gareth Jones highlight the importance of leaders demonstrating they have specialist skills and a professional hinterland that stretches beyond the realms of leadership and general management.[2] Periodic demonstrations of technical capability can help to show others in the public relations team that the leader really is 'one of them'. Such actions are a better way of demonstrating empathy and an understanding of their world than platitudes and endless stories of the trials and tribulations the leader has faced during their own career. It also positions the leader as a superior technician the team can learn key skills from.

Outside of the public relations department similar displays of technical proficiency can also help to generate credibility as well as a dialogue with different groups of employees. Goffee and Jones note this is particularly effective when dealing with colleagues who exhibit a strong sense of professional identity. This often manifests itself in a belief within the group that they make a disproportionately large contribution to the success of the organisation. This interpretation of their own worth as experts means they tend to resent the intervention of senior management. Rather than the organisation, such colleagues believe they are ultimately answerable to a higher calling, usually some form of professional association. Examples of such groups include client-facing fee earners in a professional service firm, clinicians in a hospital, research scientists in a pharmaceutical company and academics in a university. Working with such groups requires the public relations leader to demonstrate their own technical mastery. It is about establishing a peer relationship by showcasing a set of professional skills and knowledge that they do not possess.

The need to understand the nuts and bolts of the job is also driven by the reality of life within many organisations. Danny Moss, Andrew Newman and Barbara DeSanto interviewed practitioners and identified five key characteristics of the public relations managers' role in the UK.[3] These were monitor and evaluator, issues management expert, key policy and strategy adviser, trouble shooter/problem solver and, finally, communication technician. Moss and his colleagues suggest that the retention of the technician role may reflect the relatively small size of the communication departments still found in many organisations. The need for public relations leaders to roll up their sleeves is an economic necessity and this is further highlighted when it is considered that the findings of their study were published in 2005. This predates an international economic crisis that has further squeezed the resources available for communication and other strategic management disciplines. Furthermore, the research also highlights that some public relations leaders prefer to retain a close control over certain high risk technical areas such as financial communication and issues management.

A mastery of key technical skills is also important given the strategic model that sits at the heart of this book (see Chapter 5). At the functional level of strategy it is the role of public relations to liaise with the other specialist functional areas in the organisation to determine how the public relations department can contribute its specific communication skills to meet the organisation's mission and objectives. This will include delivering specific programmes and campaigns in support of these aims. At the functional level of public relations strategy, leaders need a clear understanding of the different communication channels at their disposal, as well as the tools and techniques to use them effectively. Public relations leaders not only head up departments that themselves deliver communication products and services, but also support and enable colleagues across the organisation to do the same (see the discussion of the internal educator role in Chapter 13). The ability to execute such a role requires a high level of technical competence and credibility.

What is an expert?

To better understand the technical role of the public relations leader it is helpful to explore in greater detail the nature of professional expertise and operational proficiency. A useful place to start is with an influential study conducted in the 1980s that set out to challenge the thinking behind the development of artificial intelligence in computers. In *Mind Over Machine: The Power of Human Intuition and Expertise in the Era of the Computer*, Hubert and Stuart Dreyfus challenged the assumption that humans can act intelligently only by performing as conscious, analytical problem solvers.[4] Their work specifically refuted the idea that people generally follow a linear and rational method of reasoning involving sets of formulas, rules, plans and decisions. While such an approach might be effective in situations involving well-defined tasks and solutions, Dreyfus and Dreyfus argued it is much less useful when confronting problems that are harder to define. This led them to conclude that there are different kinds of intelligent behaviour to analytical reasoning and that these are particularly prevalent amongst highly proficient individuals who are experts in their fields.

To support their case Dreyfus and Dreyfus developed a model of skills acquisition that set out to illustrate how an individual progresses from novice to expert.[5] These ideas have evolved into a wider theory of expertise and the model is still used to provide a framework for informing managerial development. The key insight to be drawn from the Dreyfus model is that context becomes increasingly important the further someone moves up the different levels of learning. For the Dreyfus brothers context and knowledge are indivisible at the level of the expert practitioner. Rather than being characterised by rules and routine, the upper echelons of the model emphasise heightened situational awareness and decision-making. It is this sensitivity to a given situation, as well as the ability to use and adapt the knowledge we have, which forms the essence of human expertise.

Bent Flyvbjerg encapsulates this thinking with the observation that 'personal experience via trial and error is more important than context-independent, explicit, verbally formulated facts and rules'.[6] Similarly, knowing when to bend or ignore the rules becomes a key facet of expertise. It is important to note, however, that inherent in this ability to be flexible must also be an appreciation of right and wrong. This, in turn, reinforces the point that ethical decision-making and judgement is bound up not only in expertise but also leadership (see Chapter 8).

This way of looking at expertise is interesting given the challenges faced by public relations leaders at the functional level of strategy. To explore the implications of these insights for practice let us now consider the realm of media relations and what it means to be a novice, intermediate and expert public relations practitioner in this field.

From novice to media relations expert

At the level of a novice the development of media relations skills tends to focus on learning and applying the protocols associated with researching, writing and distributing press releases. This activity requires good written skills, a basic appreciation of news values, knowledge of the techniques required to generate attention-grabbing communication collateral, as well as an understanding of the working habits of journalists and how to reach them. Novices tend to be told which news to promote by their direct line manager or others in the organisation. They therefore operate as the implementer in a process rather than the decision-maker. Given their inexperience novices tend to rigidly apply the rules they are taught regardless of the situation they face. The approval processes and protocols associated with the production of a press release provide a security blanket when responding to the direction of others. This means they tend to exhibit little discretionary judgement and flexibility. For example, when following up the dispatch of a press release they can be easily fazed by journalists who ask questions they have not anticipated or who maybe views the news that has been presented to them from an entirely different angle. The ability to recognise the questions and issues that may arise in such situations – and the confidence to challenge others about the course of action being recommended – only comes with experience.

The intermediate media relations specialist is more autonomous and flexible in their decision-making. They are still guided consciously by routine and a set of standard procedures (such as those associated with campaign planning and the composition of a press release) as this tends to be their way of coping with a busy and pressurised environment involving a raft of campaign activities, the assimilation of lots of information and the supervision of different people. It also helps them to keep focused on wider objectives and goals. Nevertheless, intermediate practitioners also have the confidence to deviate from established rules and processes. For example, they might be happy to informally pitch ideas to journalists over the telephone rather than go through the process of writing a press release. They are able to do this because of the knowledge they have accumulated from prior experience and their appreciation of how the news they are promoting supports the wider objectives of the organisation. They are also adept at tailoring the same material for different media and spotting emerging opportunities for coverage.

The role of the expert in media relations is qualitatively different from the novice and intermediate practitioner. It is about ensuring the practice of key technical skills – such as writing press releases, working with journalists and planning campaigns – constantly takes into account the situations and issues generated by an unpredictable, diverse and fast moving media environment. This is less to do with having the skills necessary to produce and generate communication collateral and more about the need to interpret how the different parts of the modern media universe impact on one another. This real-time analysis might involve quickly altering the tone and content of a press release in response to new developments; reconsidering the optimum time to release company news; or abandoning a campaign altogether.

To be able to manage in such situations requires a grasp of complex situations that allows the expert to move between intuitive and analytical approaches built on knowledge developed over time. Skill therefore becomes an integrated approach to professional action that incorporates both routines and the decisions linked to how, when and if to use particular approaches and methods.[7] Improvisation is also an important part of the expert's repertoire. Indeed, it serves to illustrate the very essence of expertise. The process of improvisation involves the flexible and innovative treatment of something that already exists. For example, consider the act of improvisation in jazz. The musicians involved use their technical skills to create something new in real time from an existing piece of music.[8] Faced with an uncertain and complex situation the public relations expert does the same by drawing upon what they have done in the past to guide their actions in a new and emerging situation.

The following summarises the different skill levels we have just discussed in a media relations context:[9]

Novice:
*   Reactive (instructed by others)
*   Adheres strictly to rules and guidelines
*   Applies these rules regardless of the situation

Intermediate:
*   Proactive (can spot an opportunity and respond quickly)
*   Still relies on rules and guidelines (but can go off-piste if it is expedient)
*   Understands the bigger picture

Expert:
*   Interactive (influences the thinking and practices of others)
*   No longer relies on rules, guidelines or maxims
*   An intuitive grasp of situations based on deep understanding

Making sense of the media environment

To further highlight the importance of expertise in the public relations field it is useful to consider Dawn Gilpin and Priscilla Murphy's[10] conceptualisation of the contemporary media landscape as a single complex system. The essential characteristic of a complex system is that it is made up of multiple interacting agents. In the case of the media these different agents are individuals, organisations and media outlets. Each of these agents, in turn, engages in a huge range of digital, non-digital, mass and personal communication. This notion of an integrated system is helpful because it is increasingly difficult to draw neat boundaries between what was once termed traditional and digital media. Even print and broadcast outlets are migrating to a range of digital formats at the same time as maintaining their existing channels. This reinforces Lars Qvortrup's[11] observation that digital media integrates all known media into one converged multimedia system with an unlimited system of features.

Edelman, the global public relations consultancy, has tried to make sense of this world for their clients and employees by conceptualising the modern media environment as a cloverleaf consisting of four, overlapping elements (see Figure 12.1). These overlaps further highlight why all media channels are increasingly viewed as one entity rather than as four distinct categories:[12]

*   *Traditional media* encompasses radio, TV and print media outlets. This sector includes established media brands such as the BBC, CNN, *Le Figaro* and *El País*.
*   *Hybrid media* includes media companies that have emerged in the digital age. These are largely blogs, some of which focus on niche audiences and issues while others have a more mainstream appeal. One of the best-known examples of hybrid media is the *Huffington Post*.

Navigating A New Media Ecosystem

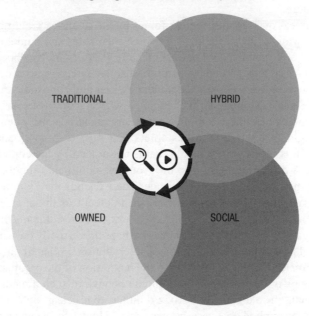

Figure 12.1 The Edelman media cloverleaf™

Source: Media Cloverleaf

- *Owned media* refers to the media channels that the organisation controls, such as its own website, blogs, podcasts and apps. Companies now have the capacity to cost effectively create content that can be instantaneously communicated to a wide range of external and internal stakeholders.
- *Social media* platforms such as Facebook and Twitter mean that content about a business is not just produced and distributed globally by the company's communication team but also by consumers, employees, partners, suppliers, communities and competitors.

It is the unpredictable nature of the interactions between these different media agents that leads to the creation of a dynamic and unstable system. For example, news of events breaks first increasingly in social media such as Twitter and Facebook. This was the case with the death of Michael Jackson in the United States and the popular uprisings that occurred in the Arab world during the spring of 2011. In such cases the initial absence of credible, independently verified information means that rumour and emotional responses can spread like a forest fire, spilling over into the comment and analysis featured on television, radio and newspapers. The instantaneous communicative capacity and reach of social media also ensures that this spiral of speculation happens more quickly than ever before.

This complex, overlapping context forces public relations practitioners to sail in uncharted waters. These are areas in which clear rules and guidelines have yet to be devised and established. For example, the Twitter and Facebook platforms that a company creates and controls might also be categorised as owned media rather than social media. As 'owned' media Twitter and Facebook are often used as an important customer-service channel where grievances are aired and disputes resolved. In these online spaces organisations are seen to have a legitimate right to interact with customers that post comments and messages about them. In contrast, social media that is not owned by the company is more problematic. A customer might post unfavourable comments about a company's products on their personal Facebook page. Their friends may join in the chorus of disapproval online. The company may then detect this dissatisfaction as part of its online monitoring activities. However, how will the company be received if it tries to engage with consumers in a place where they usually only interact with friends and family? Is this a legitimate intervention? What if the claims are inaccurate, misleading and damaging to the reputation of the organisation?

Expectations of how organisations should behave in such a media landscape are situational, problematic and fuzzy rather than clear cut. They require judgement to be applied on a case-by-case basis. However, in such a fast-moving environment the time for deliberation and reflection is significantly reduced. The traditional news cycle is dead and public relations leaders are instead faced with 24/7 speculation, comment and analysis. Furthermore, seeking answers in existing methods might be legitimate and useful but does not present practitioners with the whole picture. Too much focus on oven-ready solutions and the sort of traditional management approaches discussed in Chapter 10 can lead to decisional paralysis.[13] In this climate the essence of expertise is to be a good decision-maker, flexible and emotionally intelligent so he or she can deal with different circumstances.

This is especially important when considering the challenges generated by the different levels of strategy we discuss in Chapter 5. A heightened climate of accountability requires the public relations practitioner to shuttle between these different levels and depending on the type of organisation they work for; this might involve responding to journalist enquiries related to the impact of organisational decision-making on issues linked to the market, taxpayers, customers, overseas workers, the community or the wider public interest.

Developing and maintaining expertise

The challenges we have discussed highlight that a key facet of expertise for the leader is trying to make sense of the world for themselves and others. This sets the frame within which key technical skills are executed. However, it is impossible for one person to fully describe or understand an entity such as a complex adaptive system like the modern media environment. It requires multiple perspectives, and because the situation may change in unpredictable ways, we need repeated observations and systematic feedback from others. In such an environment interpersonal relationships become the vehicle for wisdom.[14] This highlights the need for public relations leaders to connect within and across the organisation. Developing and maintaining expertise is a social as well as an internal process. It is ongoing and dynamic. Experts develop their thinking through a dialogue with themselves as well as conversations with others. Expert knowledge is not a neat package of finely formed ideas that can be easily communicated from one person to another. Rather, it is the very act of communication that generates knowledge and expertise.[15]

These observations serve to highlight the importance of interpersonal communication skills to expertise. Just being well connected is not enough. Experts need to build and maintain relationships that are characterised by trust, reciprocity and cooperation. To build such productive relationships requires a repertoire of interpersonal skills. This involves questioning and listening skills, reflection (see Chapter 11), influencing and persuading, as well as assertiveness.[16] Furthermore, those with a good level of interpersonal skills can also perform as positive communication role models for others in the organisation and are likely to be perceived as good leaders and managers. In addition, the process of interacting with and learning from others hones the proficiency of public relations people in this area, as well as providing further opportunities for them to demonstrate their technical expertise.

Summary

Public relations is a discipline that does not have many rules. It deals in situations, the organisational character and issues such as defining and interpreting values. These are areas of practice where there are few 'rules' and this is one of the reasons why our profession is so difficult to define. Technical proficiency is one of the few ways that public relations practitioners can ground their work which is why good technical skills are so important. However, in their book *The Future of Management*, Gary Hamel and Bill Breen warn against the danger of standards and rules stifling initiative and organisational adaptability.[17] This issue strikes at the heart of why technical expertise is so important for public relations. An expert practitioner needs to continuously reflect on their practice and drive their development through ongoing engagement with others.

This is important because expertise is associated with how individuals interpret and respond to the context they operate in. It is about navigating a way through a situation rather than slavishly applying fixed methods and thinking. Expertise involves knowing when to bend or ignore the rules and how to forge your own path. However, appreciating what rules can be bent is predicated on a foundation of technical excellence. This therefore requires public relations leaders to continue to drive their personal development on technical matters, as well as what might be termed strategic leadership competencies.

Notes

1 Macnamara, J. (2012). *Public Relations: Theories, Practices, Critiques*. Frenchs Forest: Pearson.
2 Goffee, R. and Jones, G. (2007). Leading clever people, *Harvard Business Review*, 85(3), 72–9.
3 Moss, D., Newman, A. and DeSanto, B. (2005). What do communication managers do? Defining and refining the core elements of management in a public relations/corporate communication context, *Journalism and Mass Communication Quarterly*, 82(4), 873–90.
4 For an excellent summary and analysis on the work of Dreyfus and Dreyfus see Flyvbjerg, B. (2009). *Making Social Science Matter: Why Social Inquiry Fails and How It Can Succeed Again*. Cambridge: Cambridge University Press. Our own summary draws heavily on Flyvbjerg's key interpretations and insights. He also highlights the importance of the brothers' research to a key philosophical debate about the nature of knowledge that is still raging at the heart of contemporary social science.
5 Dreyfus, H.L. and Dreyfus, S.E. (1986). *Mind Over Machine: The Power of Human Intuition and Expertise in the Era of the Computer*. Oxford: Basil Blackwell.
6 Flyvbjerg, B. (2009). *Making Social Science Matter* (see above).
7 Eruat, M. (1994). *Developing Professional Knowledge and Competence*. London: Falmer Press.
8 Weick, K.E. (2001). *Making Sense of the Organisation*. Oxford: Blackwell.
9 This draws on the summary of the Dreyfus model provided by Michael Eruat. See Eruat, M. (1994). *Developing Professional Knowledge and Competence* (see above).
10 Gilpin, D.R. and Murphy, P.J. (2010). Implications of complexity theory for public relations: beyond crisis. In Heath, R.L. (ed.), *The SAGE Handbook of Public Relations* (pp. 71–83). Thousand Oaks, CA: Sage.
11 Qvortrup, L. (2006). Understanding new digital media, *European Journal of Communication*, 21(3), 345–56.
12 Gilpin, D.R. and Murphy, P.J. (2010). Implications of complexity theory for public relations (see above).
13 Bolton, M.J. and Stolcis, G.B. (2008). Overcoming failure of imagination in crisis management: the complex adaptive system, *The Innovation Journal: The Public Sector Innovation Journal*, 13(3), article 4. www.innovation.cc/scholarly-style/bolton-stolcis3dec2008v1314.pdf.
14 Weick, K.E. (2001). *Making Sense of the Organisation*. Oxford: Blackwell.
15 See Jones, R. and McKie, D. (2009). Intelligent participation: communicating knowledge in cross-functional project teams. *International Journal of Knowledge Management Studies*, 3, 180–94.
16 See Owen Hargie's definitive overview of interpersonal communication: Hargie, O. (2011). *Skilled Interpersonal Communication: Research, Theory and Practice*. Hove: Routledge.
17 Hamel, G. and Breen, B. (2007). *The Future of Management*. Boston, MA: Harvard Business School Press.

13 The internal educator

Introduction

One of the central themes of this book is that organisations are defined, constituted and enabled by communication. Organisations – and the people within them – communicate incessantly, regardless of whether they intend to or not (even a decision not to communicate is a communication decision). Indeed, it is possible to make sense of an organisation by looking at how it is represented by the people who work in it. A cheerful, welcoming and efficient receptionist immediately makes a positive impression on the visitors to an office. How a buyer deals with a supplier on the phone can speak volumes about attitudes towards the organisation's value chain. The different ways managers brief their staff on company news can suggest how much importance is placed in the organisation on internal communication. Are there regular, face-to-face updates for employees by managers, is important operational information only communicated to employees by email, or is there a mix of activity?

The logic of a communicating organisation is that communicative literacy needs to be embedded throughout the organisation. This requires the public relations leader to assume the role of an internal educator, establishing and developing the communicative ability of the whole organisation rather than just focusing on traditional communication activities.[1] In this chapter we explore what this entails and the implications it has for the conduct of public relations in the organisation. These issues are tackled under the following headings:

- Lessons from finance and human resources
- A role with five dimensions
- Touring the organisation as a cultural guide
- Developing appropriate behaviours and skills in the organisation

Lessons from finance and human resources

The holistic world of communication we have previously described requires a change in mindset in the organisation. Responsibility for stakeholder communication shifts from something that is associated just with the public relations department – and perhaps a handful of senior executives – to a general managerial competence. While all managers must communicate to carry out their job effectively by talking to colleagues, writing emails and issuing directives, what we are highlighting here is the process of organisational rather than managerial communication. This focus requires managers to think through the communicative dimensions of their activities and how they impact on stakeholders. This new responsibility is akin to the financial and human resources (HR) requirements already placed on managers by their organisations.

In the modern organisation managers are expected to control budgets, make financial projections and sign off expenses, as well as appraise, develop and discipline their people. It is seen as legitimate within organisations, and by managers themselves, that they are judged on their performance in these areas. Such skills are seen as part and parcel of management; they 'come with the territory'. The processes and support for this delegated activity are set by the organisation's finance and HR experts.

These functions have, in turn, evolved to meet this challenge. As routine finance and HR tasks have been devolved to management teams, accountants and HR professionals have focused on key strategic activities: for example, internal audit, the production of consolidated accounts and investment strategy (for finance); talent management, remuneration and recruitment policy (for HR). There is also an ongoing focus on how to enable other managers to successfully execute their finance and HR responsibilities. As Hamrefors highlights, 'a financial director is not invited to participate in leadership just because he/she is very good at bookkeeping, but because of knowledge and skills in building the financial strength of the organization'.[2] In a public relations context instead of financial strength it is influencing and shaping the communicative ability of the organisation that becomes a key a facet of leadership. The question that now needs to be considered is what does this entail in practice?

A role with five dimensions

Our model in Chapter 5 highlights that the public relations leader needs to shuttle between four levels of organisational strategy: societal, corporate, value chain and functional. Every level of strategy generates issues with a communicative dimension, usually involving colleagues from across the organisation. This means that the need to enable and empower people to operate as effective communicators also needs to cut across these four levels of strategy. This means that the role of the internal educator is concerned with more than just skills development; it is about:

- creating a communicative culture for all employees that supports the organisation's values and purpose (societal level of strategy);
- improving management decision-making by highlighting the importance of intangible assets such as reputation and relationships (corporate level);

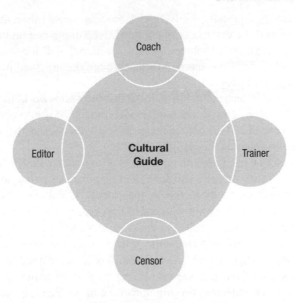

Figure 13.1 The five roles of the internal public relations educator

- better interactions with the groups and individuals that matter to the organisation (value chain);
- effective communication activities in every part of the organisation (functional).

Being an internal educator is a challenging and diverse role, involving a range of skills and competencies. We suggest that it can be sub-divided into five sub-roles as illustrated in Figure 13.1. The *cultural guide* helps to set the tone and style of communication within the organisation. The other four sub-roles are about the enactment of communication. We will now discuss the idea of communication culture and the part played by the public relations leader in developing this.

Touring the organisation as a cultural guide

Helping to build and encourage a communicative culture in the organisation is a crucial first step for the internal educator. The communicative culture will frame the environment in which all communication activities take place. In essence, this process involves trying to answer the question of how communication is done around here. What are the principles and values that govern us as communicators? While the public relations team should lead the discussions around these questions, the process should be open and participatory involving a range of internal and external stakeholders. This will generate valuable intelligence about how the organisation's existing communication is perceived by a range of groups and individuals. Such a process is also inherently educative. The purpose behind the discussions will need to be explained and debated with employees and other stakeholders. Their reactions and feedback will also challenge the public relations team to think through the practical implications of what is being asked of people.

The cultural-web technique provides a useful framework to guide these discussions.[3] We have applied the cultural web model for use in communication as shown in Figure 13.2. This considers specifically the factors that impact on an organisation's communicative culture.

This model can be used as both an audit tool (to understand the organisation's current communicative culture) and for visioning purposes (what do we want the communication culture to look like in the future). Combining both serves to highlight gaps and areas for improvement in the organisation. To do this requires those engaged in the cultural project to compose and consider a range of questions linked to the model's different elements. A list of questions that can be used for auditing purposes is highlighted below. These should be adapted to suit different organisational settings but provide an idea of the sort of issues that need to be interrogated to better understand communicative culture. These questions can also be reframed to allow people to think about what they would like the communication culture to become and how they might achieve this. For example, the first question that asks *what is the nature of the stories that circulate around the organisation* can be changed to *what stories would we like circulating around the organisation* to prompt a reflection on aspirations and future objectives.

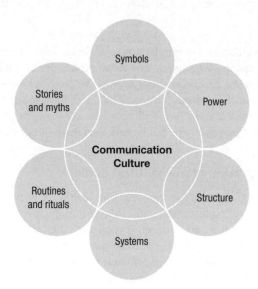

Figure 13.2 A cultural web for communication

Source: Adapted from G. Johnson (1988). Rethinking incrementalism. *Strategic Management Journal*, 9(1), 75–91

Stories and myths

*   What's the nature of the stories that circulate around the organisation? Are they associated with organisational success or failure? This can tell public relations leaders whether the organisation's grapevine is associated with good or bad news. For example:

    'Everyone is excited about the new product range.'

    'We've done what everyone said was impossible.'

    'It looks as if redundancies are on the horizon.'

    'The number of complaints coming into the call centre is rising and we can't cope.'

*   Do people talk about the organisation's history, traditions and heritage with pride? Do they identify with these stories? Are the stories used to illustrate and reinforce the organisation's culture? For example:

    'The founders risked it all and re-mortgaged everything they had, they believed passionately in this business.'

    'We were the first company to come up with this idea and we've been the market leader ever since.'

    'This place has always been run by accountants rather than engineers.'

    'We've forgotten our roots and what this organisation was set up to be.'

*   Do the stories people tell about the organisation's leaders have a communicative dimension? If they do, it is useful to reflect on what these reveal about the perceptions people have of the communication behaviours that are desired or accepted in the organisation. For example:

    'The managing director makes sure that he knows the first names of all the staff he meets in our stores.'

    'The finance director always tell us bad news to our face.'

    'Apparently, the new chief executive doesn't suffer fools gladly.'

    'The chairman is desperate for a knighthood which is why we spend so much money sponsoring these events.'

Routines and rituals

*   What sort of communication is emphasised in the organisation? Is it mostly one-way, information exchange or is dialogue encouraged amongst staff and senior management? Are employees and other stakeholders talked to, or talked with? Is communication tailored for different situations or are particular approaches and behaviours favoured over others? Is there one particular example that epitomises the organisation's approach to communication?

Symbols

*   How accessible is the language used by people in the organisation? Is there a lot of jargon and technical language circulating around the organisation?

Is this how people communicate to external stakeholders such as customers and service users? If they do, is the use of this language appropriate?

- Do recurrent buzz words and phrases circulate around the organisation? What do these say about the organisation's priorities and/or ways of operating?
- Which of its aspects does the organisation like to highlight in its communication? For example, does it emphasise research and development, customer focus, charitable donations, partnerships, its links with sport and music? Do these match the organisation's stated priorities and values? Which aspects do people think require greater emphasis?
- What visual symbols are prevalent in the organisation? Do people dress formally or informally? Do the senior-management team share an open-plan office with other employees?

Organisational structures

- Is communication centrally controlled? For example, are there formal sign-off procedures before communication activities can be initiated? What is the level of autonomy accorded to individual managers?
- Is there the scope for communication to respond to local conditions and opportunities?
- Do people feel they have enough support from the organisation to be effective communicators?

Control systems

- What communication activities are most closely controlled and monitored by the organisation? For example, is social media monitored and does the organisation respond to relevant issues that arise there? Is the website regularly updated with fresh content? Do employees receive quick and satisfactory response from questions they post on the organisation's intranet? Are relevant press cuttings circulated to staff? Is there a database that records all contact with key stakeholders?

Power structures

- What are the main blockages that prevent communication practice being changed in the organisation? Does the leadership team like things as they are? Does the leadership team and others in the organisation buy into the idea of a communicating organisation?

By considering the answers to these questions the public relations leader can begin to identify key issues in the organisation that impact on communication culture. From these insights it is helpful to identify key themes and these can be brought together in a SWOT analysis for communication. What are the current strengths of the organisation's existing communication culture (identification with key values, pride)? What are its weaknesses (senior executives do not enact the values)? Does this reveal any opportunities (the behaviour of senior executives should be seen to embody core values)? What about the threats that need to be considered (senior executives ignore and resist this requirement)? The public relations leader can use these insights to develop plans, strategies and policies that seek to address these issues.

As *the cultural guide* a public relations leader should also be an exemplar for best practice in communication. This extends beyond being responsible for the production of professional communication material. It includes ensuring that all of their activities and behaviours reinforce the communicative culture the organisation wishes to foster.

Developing appropriate behaviours and skills in the organisation

The communicative climate promoted by the public relations leader as cultural guide will manifest itself at a practical level in a range of activities linked to the other sub-roles associated with the internal educator: coach, trainer, censor and editor. The part each plays in building the communicative capacity of colleagues will now be discussed.

Coach

This role is about the public relations leader providing advice and feedback to colleagues in the organisation that is designed to improve their communicative effectiveness. It is a direct, personal and one-to-one relationship designed to help people cope with the circumstances that are specific to them. Coaching can be conducted as part of an ongoing relationship, or as a one-off exercise. For example, we would expect a public relations leader to have an ongoing coaching role with their chief executive (also see Chapter 4). This could involve providing advice prior to a meeting with a journalist, critiquing a recent broadcast interview or commenting on how the chief executive performed in a question and answer session with staff. This relationship should sit outside of the usual hierarchical chain of command. It requires the public relations leader talking to the CEO as a peer rather than as a subordinate.

The public relations leader may also develop an ongoing coaching relationship with other colleagues who are required to consistently engage with stakeholders. The finance director in a publicly listed company is an obvious example given their requirement to regularly present financial information to the media, analysts and regulators. A one-off coaching interaction might occur with a manager responsible for part of the organisation that is making people redundant. This situation requires intensive dialogue with employees, unions, the media and local as well as national politicians. In such circumstances the public relations coach and the manager are likely to work closely together until the process is complete.

In addition to tips on technical matters linked to media relations and interpersonal communication, the public relations leader as coach must also encourage communicative behaviours amongst other executives that enact the organisation's key values. For example, if the values cited include 'integrity' and 'respect' it is incumbent on managers to be even handed in their dealings with stakeholders. Going back to the case we have just cited as an illustration, those who oppose redundancies should be granted the same access to information as groups who might be neutral on the subject. If an organisation aspires to 'excellence' then it is also reasonable to assume that the people charged with overseeing a redundancy process go beyond the requirements of statutory compliance to ensure employees receive the best support and advice available.

Trainer

The public relations leader can conduct or commission training to support colleagues in a range of communication tasks. These might include media-handling skills, speech writing, making presentations, an induction on social media and communication planning, as well as how to write newsletters, press releases and blogs. Consideration can also be given to providing an online resource containing material that can be downloaded by employees such as guides, toolkits and campaign templates that provide practical advice and guidance. These can be supported by podcasts and webinars while broadcast sharing websites, such as YouTube, provide the opportunity to generate short videos on key aspects of communication for colleagues in the organisation.

Censor

This role is associated with planned communication in the organisation carried out by colleagues from outside the public relations department. A consequence of sustained discussion in the organisation about the importance of communication can be a sudden desire for people to initiate their own communication activity. Furthermore, there may be other teams who already generate their own communication collateral and have a budget for public relations. This type of activity can include isolated initiatives, such as the creation of a Facebook page for patients by a team of clinicians, or multi-faceted campaigns that use a variety of tools and techniques. An example of this would be an integrated media relations and sponsorship programme conducted by a company division to promote itself as a progressive employer in the local community.

Although some of this activity may occur outside their field of vision, it is important that the public relations team is aware of as much of this devolved communication as possible. An audit can be implemented by contacting different departments and monitoring activity. The aim is to identify planned communication activity that may have an adverse impact on the organisation's reputation and relationships. The public relations team needs to discuss the implications of such activity with the managers responsible and provide advice where appropriate. This may include a recommendation to postpone or abandon the activity entirely. For example, clinical colleagues may not have thought through the protocols and logistics associated with administering a Facebook page. They may have underestimated the time it takes to monitor activity and respond to the volume of comments posted by patients. Instead of generating expectations amongst patients that cannot be met, a prudent course of action might be to shelve the project until someone is allocated the necessary time to manage the project

The censor's advice may also extend to highlighting the unsuitability of colleagues for certain communication tasks, as well as persuading others to step forward into the spotlight. Organisational experts – such as scientists, doctors and engineers – often have higher levels of credibility with stakeholders than general managers, including the chief executive. Such expertise can be particularly helpful for reassuring stakeholders during a time of crisis, as well as for explaining complex and/or controversial issues. Such examples include the need for a product recall (scientist), the future of community health provision (doctor), or the decision to build a new highway close to an area of outstanding natural beauty (engineer).

In large organisations micro-managing all planned communication activity will not be feasible given the volume of material involved. This further reinforces the importance of developing and promoting the organisation's communicative culture and values, as well as providing accessible training materials that can support staff

Editor

The final task of the internal educator is editor. The title of this role has been selected for three reasons. First, an editor usually works with a project or idea that has been initiated by someone else. This complements the strategic raison d'être of the internal educator which is to support the work of others. Second, the editor is responsible for supervising communicative output. In the case of the organisation this will include a range of written and spoken material for use online and offline: case studies, feature articles, opinion pieces, speeches, news releases, podcasts and videos. Third, editors are the guardians of fairness, accuracy and style. They ensure that communication meets the highest professional standards.

As highly skilled technicians (also see Chapter 12) public relations leaders – with support from their teams – have the expertise to provide a range of editorial services to other departments producing their own communication material. This is, in itself, an educative process as the comments and suggestions put forward by experienced public relations practitioners can sensitise colleagues to the techniques and protocols associated with skills such as copywriting and broadcast production.

Summary

The role of the internal educator is to promote and build the organisation's communicative capacity. As such, it is a key requirement of public relations leadership. It cuts across the four levels of organisational strategy described in Chapter 5, creating a multi-faceted role that requires a range of skills and competencies. To explore these in greater detail we identify five sub-roles for the internal educator. The cultural guide seeks to provide the overarching framework that guides communication in the organisation, while the sub-roles of coach, trainer, censor and editor help to develop appropriate behaviours and skills amongst colleagues.

Notes

1 Hamrefors, S. (2010). Communicative leadership, *Journal of Communication Management*, 14(2), 141–52.
2 Hamrefors, S. (2010). Communicative leadership (see above).
3 See Johnson, G. (1988). Rethinking incrementalism, *Strategic Management Journal*, 9(1), 75–91.

14 The consultant

Introduction

This chapter is a call to action for public relations leaders to adopt a consultancy-based approach. It applies whether a practitioner is a self-employed freelancer, works in-house or for a public relations agency. The reason is simple. Good consultancy practice helps to bridge the gap between a public relations leader knowing what their strategic role should be and ensuring this is how they spend their time. It is about public relations people being listened to and others acting on their advice. Having excellent technical skills and understanding the theory around our discipline is important (see Chapter 12), but being able to apply this knowledge to a range of organisational challenges is what separates good intentions from action. Such a perspective forms one of the book's central themes: that is, public relations professionals are judged as much by how they behave as what they know and do.

A consultancy mindset is also important given the requirement discussed in Chapter 5 for the public relations leader to intervene as an adviser at different levels of organisational strategy. To operate effectively in this environment requires public relations people to adopt a range of personas and approaches. We argue that such an interactive and multi-faceted role requires a consultancy approach to be an embedded characteristic of public relations leadership. This is about bringing to the job transferable knowledge, as well as profound theoretical and practical understanding. The consultant's focus on enabling others also complements the internal educator role we discuss in Chapter 13.

These ideas and issues are discussed under the following headings:

- The Devil wears Prada
- An association with change and empowering others
- A social contract
- Building trust
- Consultancy roles
- Evaluation: happy ever after?

The Devil wears Prada

What follows is not an exhaustive guide to consultancy. There is already a wealth of useful literature available and some of this is highlighted as we go through the chapter. The aim here is to instead whet the appetite and highlight why a consultancy-based approach is particularly relevant for public relations. Our experience of working with practitioners tells us that the content will reinforce what many public relations leaders already do as they go about their business. However, by deconstructing key elements of the consultant's art our aim is to encourage reflection that improves individual effectiveness and helps leaders with the process of educating and coaching others.

It should be noted, however, that a consultancy approach on its own is not a panacea for regressive organisational cultures and practices that can inhibit the effectiveness of a public relations leader. Nevertheless, as we will seek to demonstrate, adopting a consultancy mindset can qualitatively improve their situation over time. It is also recognised that the term consultant has a public relations problem of its own. Not everyone feels comfortable with the label and the stereotype of the sharp-suited, corporate Machiavellian, which has served to obscure and devalue the benefits of an approach that can enhance rather than undermine an individual's reputation. The well-worn joke that characterises consultants as people who borrow your watch to tell you what the time is, only to then walk off with your watch and send you a bill, is typical of the sort of attitudes that have tainted perceptions. Furthermore, when the term 'consultant' is prefixed with 'public relations', practitioners can be confronted by a double credibility challenge. Such cynicism just serves to illustrate that there are bad as well as good consultants.[1] Our aim is to consider the practices of the latter.

An association with change and empowering others

A consultancy approach suits public relations. Consultants facilitate change in organisations[2] and in Chapter 3 we highlight how public relations leadership is associated with being an agent of change. This is not just about stand-alone interventions linked to high-profile change management programmes; rather the focus is also on the incremental, ongoing change that organisations need to enact to continually adapt and respond to their environment. Indeed, the role of the public relations leader is often to be a catalyst (see Chapter 11) encouraging others in the organisation to think and act differently. This might involve a one-to-one meeting with another manager to persuade them to re-consider a decision based on the impact it will have on the organisation's reputation, or it could involve the initiation of a communication campaign designed to motivate and inspire a group of people to do things differently. This affinity with change highlights the natural territory that exists between the priorities of a consultant and a public relations practitioner.

The applicability of consultancy thinking to public relations is also highlighted by the idea that consultants do not just intervene and implement solutions themselves; they also enable others. This may also be achieved through the transfer of new knowledge that enables the client to tackle the problem either now or in the future. This is an important distinction. Consultants do not always take on the delivery of a particular task. They instead work with clients to enhance their capability and capacity to do the work themselves in the future. While in practice some external consultants may wish to do the exact opposite for commercial reasons, the principle of knowledge transfer is particularly important for public relations practitioners operating as internal consultants. As discussed in Chapter 5, communication is a core organisational competence and all employees are required to build productive stakeholder relationships as part of their role. This means that the practice of public relations is embedded throughout the organisation. Given this context the public relations team needs to decide what tasks it should undertake itself and those that are delivered by others. In the latter case, the job of the public relations practitioner is to help others to effectively carry out their communicative responsibilities.

The association of consultancy with change also suggests customised, bespoke responses to organisational challenges, as well as a degree of client contact. If a public relations leader builds relationships with people in their own or another organisation, attempts to understand their business requirements, and seeks to influence them and present business solutions, then they are already operating in a consultancy role. This applies whether they work in a public relations agency and their clients are external private-sector and public-sector organisations, or they are an in-house practitioner using their knowledge and expertise to advise their own board, senior-management team and other important internal stakeholders.

This context requires consultants to have a high tolerance to ambiguity and the ability to deal with clients who say one thing and do another. Block[3] suggests that every time a practitioner gives advice to someone who is in a position to make a choice they are consulting and implicit within this definition is a notion of powerlessness.[4] The recipient of advice does not have to accept what the consultant has to say and this corresponds with the definition of a client as a person (or persons) over whom it is not possible to exercise direct control. While the consultant may have some influence over an individual, group or organisation, they do not have the ultimate power to make changes or implement programmes. As a result, consultants need a set of skills over and above their core technical expertise to get things done.

This underlines one of the key dilemmas faced by the public relations leader and emphasises the importance of a consultancy-based approach. In their expert advisory role within the organisation public relations practitioners are often working on the communicative aspects of a wider problem. Modern organisational life is complex and characterised by wicked problems[5] that can only be resolved through collaboration, shared responsibility and solutions that seek to address whole systems. For example, new customer research might reveal that there is a gap between an organisation's stated brand values and the conduct of call-centre staff. This might undermine consumer perceptions of service.

Such a problem could be due to inadequate recruitment procedures, poor training, ineffective internal communication, bad management practice, the wrong set of values, or a combination of all these factors (or something else entirely). In this context the public relations leader may have a role to play in helping to formulate a solution but is unlikely to have direct line-management responsibility for the project and all of the factors that could affect its outcome. Their effectiveness is also governed by whether or not the client, such as the senior manager with responsibility for the call centre, agrees with what is being suggested. Further difficulties may also arise if that person is not the ultimate decision-maker (it might be the human-resources director), or is just one part of a messy client eco-system in which responsibility and power is dispersed amongst a range of managers.

While the broad definition of change agent underlines the validity of linking consultancy-based practice with public relations, it is also the specific challenges this generates around ambiguity that indicate the type of coping strategies and approaches public relations leaders require. It is to these we now turn.

A social contract

A consultancy approach establishes a contract between the public relations leader and others, such as an agency client, their own chief executive or the head of a business unit in the organisation. Although this contract might involve some form of written agreement (which we'll discuss later), it is shaped essentially by a social interaction, that is, an ongoing strategic conversation through which the public relations leader contributes insight and solutions. It is essentially a fiduciary relationship in which other people put their trust in another because of the expertise they possess. This is why strategic understanding, as well as the technical expertise discussed in Chapter 12 is so important to public relations leaders. What this relationship means is that instead of being a service provider instructed by the client, the public relations leader makes judgements about what is important from their perspective, how they should use their time and where they can best add value. It is a way of working that can help the public relations leader move onto the front foot, respond strategically, demonstrate their professionalism and say 'no' where appropriate. In short, a consulting mindset can be thought of as a business model that frames the way the public relations practitioner interacts with others.

Although driven by the need to remain in control of their own destiny, it is vitally important that this social interaction with the client demonstrates empathy. This is a key principle of consultancy and, to borrow the insight expressed in Joe South's song lyric, the public relations leader should walk a mile in the shoes of the client. Do they have a clear understanding of their client's responsibilities and to whom they are accountable? What are their key internal and external relationships (a quick mapping exercise is a useful way of collating this type of information)? Does the public relations person know specifically what their client's key performance indicators are? How is their performance judged and evaluated? Through a consideration of these questions the public relations leader can begin to understand the client's world and their pressures.

Consultants need to come up with their own sense of the problem and this might be the most important thing they do in the project. Maister notes that this deeper understanding comes from a very straightforward activity, listening to clients, and he suggests a number of mechanisms to achieve this.[6] For example, it is useful to think of the first meeting with the client as a think tank. This encourages the public relations leader to explore the problem with the client. In this context, the client should be encouraged to do most of the talking and this is the place where the public relations practitioner has the opportunity to demonstrate their active listening skills.[7] By collaboratively developing the project's terms of reference the public relations practitioner not only begins to develop buy-in and trust but can also highlight what is non-negotiable.

It is also important to have a view of the client's likes and dislikes. This entails how they like to process information.[8] Some people may prefer to informally talk through the key ideas in a document during a meeting rather than reading it beforehand. Others might want the exact opposite and be annoyed if they have not had the chance to digest and mull over a report before meeting. It is also worth considering whether people prefer different presentation formats such as graphics and models rather than too much written material. Asking people how they like to work in such situations can boost effectiveness and save a lot of time. Such awareness also extends to which communication channels they prefer or – even more importantly – dislike. For instance, the client may have had a bad public-speaking experience so asking them to facilitate a programme of staff engagement road shows may meet with some resistance.

The need to step back and analyse how the client views the world may seem like common sense when presented on the page but is often overlooked in practice. A key part of being an effective consultant is having the ability to convince others that a recommended course of action is the right solution. Winning this battle for hearts and minds is not just about accumulating relevant data but being able to contextualise these insights in a way that is empathetic to the client's current situation.

This leads us to what is often the first test of the consultant–client relationship: the response to the client's brief. With 50 years of combined experience in public relations practice we can count on the fingers of both hands the number of good written briefs we have received from clients. Like the snow leopard that roams the mountain ranges of Central Asia good client briefs are seldom seen. This situation occurs despite attempts to educate clients with the provision of briefing templates requiring them to answer a series of key questions. The temptation to forensically deconstruct a briefing document can be overwhelming but the public relations leader also needs to be sensitive to how the client feels about someone interrogating their work. It can make them feel stupid, insecure, threatened, exposed and impatient. In many cases the client will not have factored in enough time for the briefing process, are not used to the process and just want you to get on with the task in hand as they see it. They may even become suspicious and wonder if another organisational agenda is influencing the public relation leader's approach to their problem. In short, it is possible to superficially win the 'battle of the brief' in a face-to-face encounter due to greater expertise but that does not mean the client will be a convinced and willing partner. How might the public relations leader overcome this challenge?

Building trust

As part of a study that examined how public relations practitioners might evaluate the impact of their programmes on the quality of stakeholder relationships, Linda Hon and James Grunig identified four elements that are essential to the quality of a relationship.[9] Their insights are also useful when considering how a public relations leader might nurture and develop a successful client relationship even if it gets off to a rocky start. It is proposed, therefore, that by linking Hon and Grunig's four indicators to key facets of consultancy practice it is possible to identify a repertoire of responses that can promote productive client partnerships.

1. *Control mutuality*: the degree to which both parties in a relationship are satisfied with the amount of control they have over a relationship.

This highlights the importance of good process. For example, a written service level agreement (SLA) can be a more effective way of kick-starting a relationship than immediately asking for a brief. This sets out the responsibilities of both the public relations team and the client. Crucially, it details what the public relations practitioner requires from the client's brief in formulating the strategic plan (see Chapter 10). This will include an understanding of the project's strategic aims, desired outcomes, agreed milestones for feedback and clear sign-off procedures, as well as conflict resolution mechanisms such as regular reviews of progress. This exercise is inherently educative and need not take a lot of time. The SLA can be a standard document that can be used for any brief but which allows the public relations practitioner to take the initiative in a negotiation by setting out for discussion what is expected of both parties. This is both reassuring for the client and helps to set their expectations.

Good consultants generally possess effective process skills. They can effectively manage a client meeting, using this to gauge the current situation, identify problems and opportunities, and – most importantly – identify the client's implicit and explicit needs at a given point in time. The public relations leader might also consider establishing user groups and networks, setting up team briefs or holding reverse seminars. They will also need to be prepared which includes being armed with new information and insights that can stimulate the discussion, as well as presenting options.

2.   *Trust*: the level of confidence each party has in the other. That is, the ability to carry out what you say.

The public relations leader's track record and reputation as a practitioner is important in this regard. Good consultants reassure their clients by telling them about the relevant experience they bring to the brief. This is not about delivering a formal credentials presentation; rather it involves reinforcing points with relevant anecdotes and stories from previous projects or including a pertinent case study with the strategic plan. While public relations agencies are often adept at this, many in-house practitioners assume that others in the organisation already know what they have done, or that it is not important because they are automatically commissioned to do the work. This misses an important opportunity. Confidence is generated by promoting the expertise that is embedded in the public relations department.

Good consultants also demonstrate excellent knowledge, quality of thinking and connections. They do not only know what is happening in the sector and the comparative positioning of the organisation but also seek to understand what is going on in the wider world and its impact. Most importantly, they are able to contextualise this knowledge for the task in hand. Why is this research relevant to the brief? What can the characteristics of this stakeholder group tell us about who we are now trying to engage? Why might this relationship support our cause? Client trust is dependent upon an umbilical cord that links this expertise and insight with the task that is at the front of their minds.

3.   *Commitment*: the extent to which both parties believe that the relationship is worth spending energy on. Is the outcome worth the effort?

If followed correctly, a consultancy driven approach to a particular public relations challenge should ensure commitment from both sides. First, it should be prized by clients for helping to make a cost-effective and tangible difference to the organisation's strategic objectives. It should also optimise the communication effort by ensuring that activity is joined up, achieves results, positions the organisation for the future and enhances the organisation's – and individual client's – reputation. In turn, it is important for the public relations team because it should reinforce their strategic knowledge, secure an important relationship and ensure an effective and efficient response to the brief. It also allows public relations practitioners to demonstrate their professionalism and enhance their reputation while generating developmental benefits: it gets them working on the things that are important, interesting and motivating.

Energy, drive and initiative are also an important part of this equation. Working with the public relations team should be a stimulating and educating experience for the clients they work with. This is where what we call 'thinking of you' moments are important. That is, the email or point in a meeting where the public relations team provide the client with a news article, campaign case study, piece of research, or the details of an event they might be interested in. These do not need to be directly related to the project that is being worked on, their importance lies in helping to add value to the client's interactions with public relations practitioners.

4.   *Satisfaction*: this is when each party believes that the other is engaging in positive steps to maintain the relationship.

Once again, process plays a key role in maintaining this element of trust, particularly the requirement for regular feedback. The project might only make up a small proportion of the public relations practitioner's overall work load but the client still needs to feel that it is moving forward. The demands of leadership make many public relations practitioners over-reliant on email communication. If geography and budget rule out face-to-face meetings then it is important to regularly speak to clients on the phone. Otherwise, it is necessary to visit the client at every opportunity, encourage working lunches and involve other team members where possible. People cooperate and work better when they come together face-to-face in a physical setting. Indeed, the frequency of all this type of contact should be specified in the SLA.

Consultancy roles

Our strategic model in Chapter 5 highlights that the public relations leader has a range of roles and a key challenge is how to shuttle constantly between the operational requirements of each. We believe that viewing different activities as a particular type of consultancy role will help the public relations leader to focus on what their contribution to a project should be, the expectations placed on them and how they should manage their time. To illustrate this point, we put forward four consultancy roles to highlight specific requirements and challenges. These use the same titles as the strategic roles highlighted in Chapter 5 with the aim of providing another way of viewing the key attributes of public relations leadership linked to implementer, catalyst, navigator and orienter.

Implementer

Even senior public relations practitioners with large teams are required to personally take on technical communication tasks (also see Chapter 12 for a more in-depth discussion of the technical role of public relations leaders) and in the implementer role they will be commissioned by a range of different clients. For example, writing a speech for the chief executive on the organisation's new values, working with the finance director to brief the media on company results, or organising the chairman's confidential meeting with a government minister to discuss corporate governance issues. In such cases the role of the leader as implementer usually requires a high degree of direct client contact but essentially involves the delivery of a standard process. While the public relations leader is likely to spend time discussing each project in some depth with the client (chief executive, finance director and chairman), the activity itself will be underpinned by the knowledge acquired from carrying out similar tasks in the past. The public relations leader, based on the brief they receive from the client, contextualises and applies this knowledge to fit the situation. It is this technical expertise grounded in situational sensitivity on which the public relations leader is judged by their clients.

Catalyst

In this role the public relations leader oversees the delivery of communication activity but does not execute directly the implementation of the task themselves. This might involve supervising a team of junior colleagues or commissioning an external supplier with either the skills or capacity they do not have. For example, there might be a problem with staff retention in one part of the organisation. Research may show that one of the reasons for this is poor employee communication. In this situation the public relations leader as catalyst could oversee a staff-engagement programme delivered by their department or advise on the appointment of a consultancy with internal communication expertise. In this role the leader acts as a catalyst by bringing people together to deliver a clearly defined programme of action. The catalyst is judged on their ability to select and manage the right team but have a degree of vulnerability as they rely on the efficiency and competence of others. In common with the implementer, the core communication activity tends to follow a standard process and way of doing things. In the case just described this could include the use of social media to engage staff, the launch of a newsletter and a programme of events. If the project does not run smoothly, the leader can expect to spend a lot of time and energy reassuring the client and fire-fighting.

Navigator

In this role the public relations leader swims in more uncertain waters. Whereas the catalyst addresses an issue that is clearly defined, the navigator deals with the opposite. Their job is to find a way through a landscape of complex, ill-defined problems. For example, a recent stakeholder survey reveals that employee engagement with the public is not living up to the organisation's core values. The job of the leader in this context is to work with the client to interrogate the issue and try to identify a programme of action that can start to address the problem. This might involve commissioning research on employee attitudes to the brand and running a pilot communication project linked to its findings. This type of communication challenge requires a high degree of client contact for the pubic relations leader and a customised rather than a standard solution.

Orienter

Here the public relations leader is using their expertise to deal with a big and self-evident problem. It is about keeping a cool head, as well as a clear sense of purpose and direction. A good example is the need for a company to recall a product and the impact this will have on key stakeholder relationships. Based on their experience and expertise the public relations leader will counsel the executive team and recommend a course of action, then go away and deliver what is required with their support where necessary. Given the problem is self-evident and requires swift action this role tends to require a lower degree of client contact than the navigator. The scale of the problem being tackled usually requires a bespoke solution with the leader playing a hands-on role.

The different consultancy roles that have been outlined require the public relations leader to move between formulaic and commoditised practice, to highly customised and intensive counsel. In each context it is important to consider the different expectations that clients will attach to these roles as these frame how they will view the adequacy of the leader's response.

Evaluation: happy ever after?

One of the key ways in which effective consultants evaluate a project is whether the future is secured and whether advocacy has been achieved. That is, is there more work on the way of the type the consultant wants and is their client now an evangelist for how they do business? Similarly, the client will primarily be concerned with whether the desired objectives were met. That is why good consultants are concerned with the impact of their work rather than just the level of activity they have carried out (see the discussion of evaluation in Chapter 10). The client will also be interested in whether it was a positive experience. Bound up in this is whether the consultant met the service-level agreements in a professional manner. The quality of the client experience helps to put goodwill in the bank which is important when things go wrong (as they inevitably will) or times get tough. Such outcomes require good interpersonal skills and energy levels, as well as the necessary knowledge and expertise to get the job done.

It is also worth considering what the client's specific expectations are around particular elements of service quality. At the beginning of a project it is useful to ask clients to identify and articulate the aspects of service quality that are most important to them. For example, their priorities might include reliability (the public relations team always delivers tasks on time and budget), responsiveness (all emails are answered within one working day) and access (the public relations leader is present at all monthly meetings to discuss progress). Asking the client for feedback at the end of a project on their perceptions of performance on each of these measures generates not just a measure of client satisfaction but also flags up potential issues that are impacting on service quality. These might include an unsustainable workload for the public relations team or poor working practices linked to time and relationship management.

By initiating this exercise at the start of the process, it is to also possible to help set and manage expectations. A common issue for leaders is a lack of time and managing the expectations of others around involvement in a project is vital.

What the process we have discussed does is provide insights that can help leaders to strike a balance between what is wanted and the art of the possible. It helps them understand and operate in a zone of tolerance: that is, the area between an adequate level of service and the client's desired level of service. The difference between the two is shaped by expectations and perceptions and this can be explored by asking the sort of direct questions we have just highlighted.

Summary

The chapter began with some negative perceptions surrounding the notion of consultancy. It ends with another. A charge that is levied against consultants is they can appear arrogant. This might have something to do with the fine dividing line that exists between having too great a sense of your own importance and being confident of your own abilities. Effective consultants should be confident as they have knowledge and skills that are important to the organisation. This confidence born of insight is also one of the reasons why they are able to develop peer relationships regardless of organisational-chart protocols. The ability to develop such relationships is particularly crucial to the effectiveness of the public relations practitioner as their strategic role should give them a licence to roam around the organisation (see Chapter 5). Consultancy thinking also allows public relations leaders to make judgements about how they use their time by working their clients through an agenda that establishes goals, agrees ways of working and defines clear outcomes. Indeed, a key facet of leadership is deciding what should occupy your time and a consultancy approach helps leaders to do that in a credible and effective manner.

Notes

1 Kotler, P. (2003). *Marketing Insights from A to Z: 80 Concepts Every Manager Needs to Know*. Chichester: John Wiley & Sons.
2 Cockman, P., Evans, B. and Reynolds, P. (1999). *Consulting for Real People: A Client-centred Approach for Change Agents and Leaders*. London: McGraw Hill.
3 Block, P. (1999). *Flawless Consulting: A Guide to Getting Your Expertise Used*. San Francisco: Jossey-Bass/Pfeiffer.
4 It might also be argued that this situation may also generate a feeling of powerfulness in some situations because the consultant does not have to suffer the consequences of their advice.
5 The first systematic conceptualisation of wicked problems can be found in Rittel, H. and Webber M. (1973). Dilemmas in a general theory of planning, *Policy Sciences*, 4, 155–9. These scholars were motivated by the realisation that many public-policy challenges cannot be addressed by adopting a traditional and linear problem-solving approach. Their insights were applied to other areas of social planning; see Roberts, N.C. (2000). Wicked problems and network approaches to resolution, *International Public Management Review*, 1(1), 1–19. Conklin built on this work by developing the idea of wickedness for the private sector; see Conklin, J. (2006). *Dialogue Mapping: Building Shared Understanding of Wicked Problems*. New York: Wiley.
6 Maister, D.H. (1997). *Managing the Professional Services Firm*. New York: Free Press.

7 For some interesting insights that explore listening theory and research see Wolvin, A.D. (ed.) (2010). *Listening and Human Communication in the 21st Century.* Chichester: Wiley-Blackwell.
8 See Nadler, D. (2005). Confessions of a trusted counsellor, *Harvard Business Review,* 83(9), 68–77.
9 Hon, L.C. and Grunig, J.E. (1999). Guidelines for measuring relationships in public relations. Paper can be downloaded from www.instituteforpr.org/topics/measuring-relationships/.

15 Public relations at the edge

Looking back and looking forward

We are told that a week is a long time in politics. In public relations we know that a day can transform the fortunes of an organisation. Reflecting on just two things that have happened in the last five years brings into sharp focus the very different world in which we now operate and the opportunities that this provides for the future.

Five years ago organisations operated in a relatively benign environment, certainly in the Western world. Then came the financial crisis the impacts of which have affected the whole global community. Furthermore, five years ago Twitter and social media generally were being used by just a few innovators and early adopters. Now they are part of the fabric of human life for billions of people. The massive challenges posed by changes in the organisational environment and the developments in communication technology have brought public relations into a new and sharp focus. Its importance to the well-being of organisations is increasingly understood by chief executives as they deal with the implications of a dynamic operational context. This context is growing ever more complex and brings with it new accountabilities and vulnerabilities in a global, interconnected, interdependent and technology enabled stakeholder world.

The flexibility of the four-by-four model

The four-by-four model that we have explored in this book is context neutral. It worked five years ago as we were beginning to develop it and it works now: that is its strength. It is impossible to know what will happen to the world of organisations and public relations in the future and any prediction of trends will be quickly outdated. However, what we do know is that organisational life will become more complicated and more accountable and that there will be an increasing number of communication channels and tools at the disposal of stakeholders and public relations professionals. We also know that public relations will be a more valued asset in any new world. Increasingly organisations will be defined and constituted by the nature of their communicative efforts whether they are by formal and informal communication or as expressed through their structures, processes and systems. We believe the model that we have proposed and the implications we have examined throughout this book will be as current in five years' time as they are now. The reasons for this are quite simple. Whatever the shape of organisations in the future, the four levels of strategy and accountability that we have defined will apply. We should explain.

Organisations will always have a relationship, a responsibility and an accountability to society as a whole, and if anything this will increase. We have articulated how public relations can help to determine the purpose and role of the organisation in society. Organisational leaders will always have to take decisions for the organisation as a whole and these decisions need to be enlightened through the intelligence that the public relations leader can bring. Organisations will always have dependencies, a value chain with whom they will have close relationships and wherever there are relationships there will be a role for public relations to protect and enhance them. There will always be a need for organisations to have organised public relations, with professionals of the highest capability advising others and developing and implementing public relations programmes which build and defend the organisation.

Running like DNA through these levels there will also always be some permanent requirements that public relations professionals need to take account of as they enact their leadership role. They will need a deep and profound understanding of the brand having been involved in its development. Public relations and communication will progressively become a crucial core competence of organisations as they interact more closely and directly with an ever-expanding set of empowered stakeholders. It is also apparent that public relations will have an unparalleled opportunity to demonstrate leadership within organisations. Indeed, communication is the essence of leadership which is why it is required in abundance in the public relations leader. The ability to plan strategically and to contribute to strategic planning at all levels within the organisation will remain a characteristic of public relations leaders just as it has characterised those many senior professionals who we have worked with over the years and marks them out from those who prefer to maintain a purely technical role.

The model has and will prepare public relations leaders to take on four mission-critical roles within the organisation: that of orienter – being the compass and true north of the organisation; navigator – keeping it in balance and stable as it negotiates choppy and conflicting stakeholder waters; catalyst – being the grit in the oyster to ensure that the organisational reality matches the organisational rhetoric; and the implementer – the expert technician whose knowledge and skill is a lever to influence and credibility in the organisation.

The core characteristic

If we were to identify just one core characteristic above all others which marks out the public relations leader, we would summarise it as contextual intelligence. This contextual intelligence is demonstrated in three ways.

First, at the macro level, the public relations leader is the chief contextual intelligencer for the whole organisation: the organisational seer and antennae who understands what is going on in the world and who bases their knowledge on facts and data but also on emotional intelligence about social trends and organisational stakeholders. The public relations leader is guardian of the organisational crystal ball, who sees round corners, who predicts issues and is massively connected to the zeitgeist.

Second, the public relations leader has contextual intelligence about their own organisation. They are immersed in its culture, structures, processes and systems and are the fixer in chief of those things that will impact on the organisation's relationships and reputation. They are the guardian of the organisation's values, have a strong ethical base and are unafraid to elevate challenges and opportunities to senior management.

Finally, public relations leaders have a deep understanding of themselves, of their role and required behaviours. They understand that to rise to the opportunities that are currently presented skills and knowledge are not enough. They have to exhibit qualities of leadership and integrity which are models within the whole organisation.

This book has focused on what we regard as the three fundamentals that make the public relations leader. They need a clear and profound understanding of the strategic contribution that public relations makes to their organisations. They require focus on a number of core preoccupations which then provide them with an authoritative, authentic and compelling voice within the organisation. Then, as experts and leaders in their field, they have a set of responsibilities which, when discharged at the highest level of competence, position them as indispensable to their organisations.

And finally...

We recommend our book to you in the hope that our thoughts prove to be of use. They have been developed over many years of practice in and reflection on what we believe to be the most exciting business discipline there is. So, we will end on a note of thanks to all our fellow professionals who have stimulated our thinking, challenged us, given us opportunities and encouraged us in our endeavours.

Index

Note: Page numbers in **bold** type refer to **figures**; page numbers in *italic* type refer to *tables*; page numbers followed by 'n' refer to notes.